2/96 **DATE DUE**

MAR 2 9 1996	JAN 2 5 2000
MAY 4 1996	FEB 1 5 2000
MAY 1 8 1996	AUG 2 8 2000
JUN 1 0 1996	FEB - 9 2001
DEC 0 7 1996	JUL 1 7 2002
FEB 1 5 1997	JUN 3 0 2003
JUN 1 4 1997	
NOV 2 2 1997	NOV 0 9 2004
JUL 0 6 1998	DEC 0 3 2005
SEP 1 6 1998	
NOV 2 8 1998	
DEC 1 8 1998	
MAY 1 5 1999	
JUL 3 1 1999	FM 407 (1/86)

HOW THE U.S. GOVERNMENT WORKS

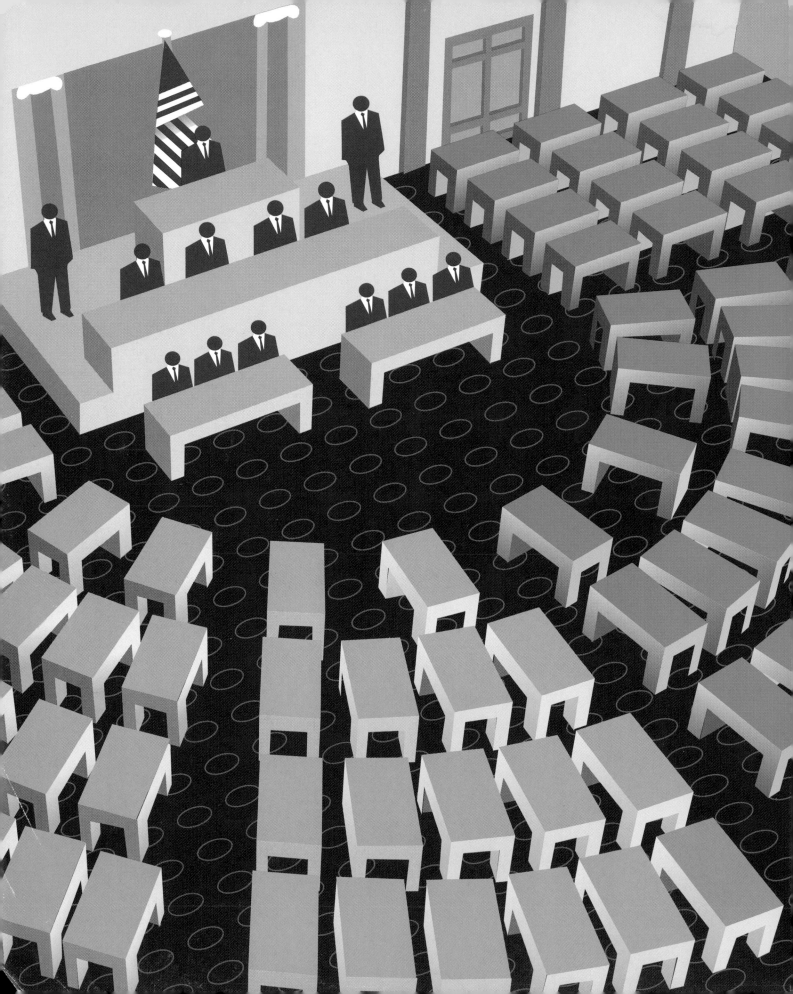

HOW THE U.S. GOVERNMENT WORKS

NANCY GENDRON HOFMANN

Illustrated by
PAUL CARBO

Ziff-Davis Press
Emeryville, California

Editor	Mary Johnson
Technical Reviewer	Michael Gross
Project Coordinator	Cort Day
Proofreaders	Carol Burbo and Nicole Clausing
Cover Illustration	Paul Carbo
Cover Design	Regan Honda
Book Design	Carrie English
Technical Illustration	Paul Carbo
Word Processing	Howard Blechman
Page Layout	Bruce Lundquist
Indexer	Kayla Sussell

Ziff-Davis Press books are produced on a Macintosh computer system with the following applications: FrameMaker®, Microsoft® Word, QuarkXPress®, Adobe Illustrator®, Adobe Photoshop®, Adobe Streamline™, MacLink®*Plus*, Aldus® FreeHand™, Collage Plus™.

If you have comments or questions or would like to receive a free catalog, call or write:
Ziff-Davis Press
5903 Christie Avenue
Emeryville, CA 94608
1-800-688-0448

ISBN 1-56276-294-X

Manufactured in the United States of America
10 9 8 7 6 5 4 3 2 1

**To Mom, Dad, Bruce,
and Brian**

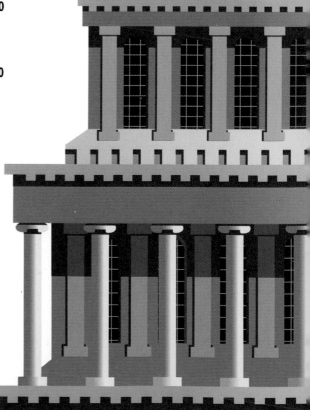

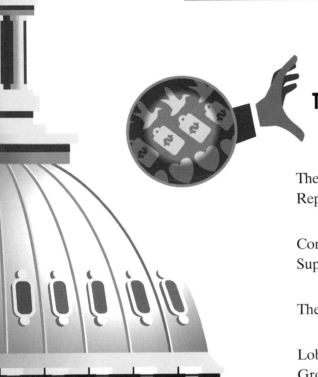

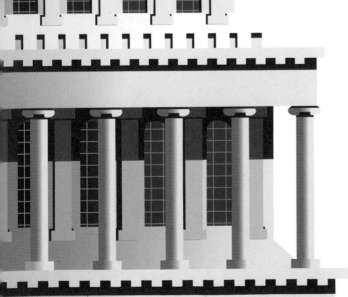

Many at Ziff-Davis Press contributed greatly to the successful completion of this book. I greatly appreciate all of your efforts. Heartfelt thanks go to Eric Stone, who took a chance on a first-time author and stood firm behind this project despite the countless ups, downs, and false starts. The patience and encouragement of editor Mary Johnson was invaluable throughout what became a more challenging project than any of us had imagined.

Illustrator Paul Carbo contributed substantially to the appeal of this book. Paul, every time I opened a package of your illustrations I was absolutely thrilled and astonished with the incredible transformation from my barest of stick-figure sketches to finished illustrations that not only made the subject matter more understandable, but had *pizzazz* as well. Thank you!

Without the experience gained from working with three members of Congress, I never would have been in a position to compose a book on the workings of our government. Thanks to The Honorable David Camp and former U.S. Representative Bill Schuette of Michigan, who helped me get my foot in the door. For three exhilarating and rewarding years as a member of his Washington staff, I will always be grateful to the late Congressman Dean A. Gallo of New Jersey.

There is little that has not already been said about the basic workings of our government. Throughout the writing of this book, I referred regularly to countless general textbooks in order to consider a variety of opinions on the same subject, and remain within the confines of a tightly knit outline. Informational materials compiled by the staff of *Congressional Quarterly* and the Congressional Research Service were just as helpful to me in writing this book as they were during my days as a congressional staffer—and kept me in touch with the Hill, even though I now live in Arizona.

I would especially like to thank my brother, Bruce Gendron, for introducing me to Eric Stone, serving as the voice of reason when all seemed lost, and for loaning me the computer and printer on which this book was written.

The world inside the beltway is not a mysterious place where people communicate in a secret language known only to Washington insiders. Just as in every other field, there is terminology specific to government and established ways of conducting the nation's business. Don't laugh, this is not a reference to the seamier side of politics that the media finds so irresistible!

More than ever before, stories of government action (or inaction), elections, and day-to-day politicking dominate the news. If you've become curious as to whether things really are as straightforward (or as scandalous) as they appear, the information contained within these pages should give you enough basic knowledge to develop your own conclusions.

Through the text and illustrations, this book explains the fundamental workings of the federal government, although many of the topics covered in this book are complex and have been the subject of exhaustive books of their own.

Unlike many other topics, the portrayal of government can easily lend itself to conservative or liberal interpretations. *How the U.S. Government Works* leans (hopefully!) neither left nor right, but stays pretty much in the middle.

Consider this book to be your user's guide to the government. It will lead you through the White House, Congress, and Supreme Court. You'll also take some interesting side trips that might even make you feel like something of a Washington insider.

1

AN OVERVIEW

Contents

READERS, IF YOU REMEMBER little more about your introductory course on the American government than the power naps and doodles that transformed founding fathers into creatures from another planet, you are not alone! In fact, intelligent Americans differ greatly both in their knowledge of government and in how much they really need to know from a practical standpoint.

Throughout the course of this book, we will explain in some detail the three branches of government—how they function independently and together—and the important role played by the American people. It is not imperative that readers proceed through the book from cover to cover. In fact, the information will probably be more useful if you take a good look at Part 1 and Chapter 1 and then pick and choose what interests you. For example, when the evening news does a story on how interest groups have made or broken the chances for passage of a particular piece of legislation, take a look at the chapters on lobbyists and interest groups and how bills are made into laws.

The benefits of learning about government in this way are numerous: It's relatively painless. You'll remember key points and processes far more easily than if you tried to memorize every chapter. Perhaps most fun of all will be your newfound ability to impress friends and family with your astute understanding of the U.S. government—a subject they may (sheepishly) admit to knowing little about!

With that in mind, let us begin our discussion of how our government works by taking a quick look at what government is, and why we have it. A few lines from two important and revered documents, the Declaration of Independence and the Constitution of the United States, neatly outline the purpose and goals of government. Despite the passage of more than two centuries, these documents continue to serve as the basis for our government today.

The Declaration of Independence states that to secure "certain unalienable rights," governments are "instituted among Men, deriving their just Powers from the Consent of the Governed...."

The purpose of the U.S. government is broadly defined in the preamble of the Constitution of the United States: "*We the People* of the United States, in Order to form a more perfect Union, establish Justice, insure domestic Tranquility, provide for the common defence, promote the general Welfare, and secure the Blessings of Liberty to ourselves and our Posterity, do ordain and establish this Constitution for the United States of America."

The Constitution was written to promote the goals outlined in the preamble. In order to accomplish these goals, a governmental structure was developed that provided for three separate but equal branches. Each branch is granted powers of its own and powers that are shared with the other branches. Underlying this structure is the basic premise that a democracy cannot function without the public's support and participation.

Structure, Powers, and Electoral Miscellany

THE STRUCTURE OF our representative government is set forth in a document known as the Constitution of the United States. The Constitution provides for three separate but equal branches of government (executive, legislative, and judicial) that have both individual and shared powers. These three branches make, execute, and interpret the laws that govern all of us. The federal government must be strong enough to act in the face of problems, respond to the wishes of the public, and carry out those wishes, but it is structured so that no one faction can take control over the others.

The system of shared and separate powers has both costs and benefits. Structuring the three branches so that each is given some role in the affairs of the others ensures that bargaining and compromise will occur, but it can also lead to deadlock and makes it difficult to pinpoint just who is responsible for government action (or lack of action). The many opportunities the public has to gain access to the federal government give everyone the opportunity to have a voice in policy making, but public involvement also slows the process considerably.

Overall, the structure of the U.S. government was designed to ensure that the collective will of the people would be given thorough consideration by policy makers and that, by forcing compromise within the legislative bodies, change would be moderate and occur slowly.

The president, senators and representatives, and the judiciary all differ in their constituencies, methods of election or appointment, and terms of office. This—and a host of other checks and balances—helps to ensure that each branch remains independent from the others and that it is impossible for a powerful faction to take control of the entire government in a single election.

The president represents all Americans and is formally elected through a uniquely American institution known as the electoral college (discussed in greater detail in Chapter 3). Presidential elections occur every fourth year, and presidents are limited to a maximum of two terms in office by the Twenty-second Amendment to the Constitution.

Members of Congress are directly elected by residents of their "home" states. Each of us is represented in Congress by two senators and one representative. The number of terms that members of Congress may serve is not limited by the Constitution. However, backed by strong public sentiment, some states have passed proposals that limit the number of terms their federal legislators may serve.

Both of the senators from a state represent *all* the residents of that state. A senator's term of office is six years, and a different third of the Senate is up for reelection every second year. Normally, only one Senate seat in each state is open during a given election. In the event of an unexpected vacancy (for example, when a senator accepts a cabinet nomination or dies in office), a special election is held to fill the unexpired term, and the state's governor may appoint a senator to serve until the special election is held. Should the special election coincide with the regular election, voters are then in a position to elect both of their senators that year.

Representatives (or congressmen and -women, as we commonly call them) are elected by a portion of their state's residents who live within a specified congressional district (for more on congressional districts, please refer to Chapter 11). Representatives serve two-year terms, and all 435 seats in the House of Representatives are open for reelection every other year.

Members of the federal judiciary (Supreme Court justices and lower federal court judges) are not elected but are appointed by the president with the advice and consent of the full Senate. Their term is for life, assuming "good behavior." Federal judges can be removed from office through impeachment by Congress, although it is an arduous process.

Here is a brief look at the three branches:

Executive Branch   The president heads the executive branch. He serves as both our symbolic and political leader, dual leadership roles that are often held by separate individuals in other countries. The powers of office, combined with the considerable economic, political, and military might of the United States, make our president one of the world's most visible and powerful leaders.

In addition to serving as our nation's chief executive, the president plays a key legislative role. Not only does he work in conjunction with Congress, he makes many legislative proposals of his own. Because he represents the entire country and has easy access to the media, the president can command the public's attention (and often support) for his legislative agenda.

To help achieve his goals, the president has carefully selected personal staff members and appointees, such as his cabinet members, who are responsible for providing him with advice and coordinating executive branch activities.

While the president and his cabinet are the most visible facets of the executive branch, by far the largest portion of this branch is the vast work force collectively known as "the bureaucracy." The federal bureaucracy conducts the day-to-day business of government by executing the laws that are made by Congress and signed by the president.

Legislative Branch   The government's legislative and oversight branch, or Congress, is divided into two different and equally powerful chambers—the Senate and the House of Representatives. Congress reviews existing policies and programs and makes our laws (which are subject to the president's approval). To address the practically limitless variety of issues (some are controversial, most are not) that come under the jurisdiction of Congress, members of both houses divide into specialized committees.

Of the three branches, the legislative branch is the most accessible to the public. Members of Congress are directly elected by their constituents and must remain accessible to them in order to stay abreast of constituent needs, serve their interests—and stay in office.

The public can observe the Senate and House in action from visitors' galleries in each chamber (except for the occasional closed session). Most committee meetings and hearings are also open to the public. C-SPAN, a relatively recent development, has brought both floor and committee proceedings into the living rooms of millions of cable television subscribers.

Readers who have done research at the Library of Congress, ordered documents published by the Government Printing Office, or taken a tour of the U.S. Capitol or Botanical Garden might be surprised to learn that these institutions are also within the legislative branch's jurisdiction.

Judicial Branch   The "supreme law of the land" (composed of the Constitution and laws and treaties made pursuant to the Constitution) is upheld by members of the federal judiciary. This supreme law binds all judges in our country and takes precedence over any individual state's constitution or laws. It is the president who is charged with enforcing these laws, through his executive power.

The judicial branch and the public are somewhat isolated from one another. Insulating federal judges from political and public pressures helps to ensure their independence.

Only in a relatively small way can the public have an influence on the judicial branch. By voting for president, the people select an individual who is likely to view issues in a way similar to their own. Should a vacancy occur in the Supreme Court or other federal court, it is reasonable for the people to expect that the president would try to appoint a judge with political views that are comparable to his own. Opportunities for change in the make-up of the bench occur with far less frequency than they do in the offices of the president or Congress. The filling of a vacancy on the Supreme Court never fails to generate considerable excitement and interest across the nation.

Structure of the Federal Government

THE CONSTITUTION

LEGISLATIVE BRANCH

THE CONGRESS

Senate   House

Architect of the Capitol
United States Botanical Garden
General Accounting Office
Government Printing Office
Library of Congress
Office of Technical Assessment
Congressional Budget Office
Copyright Royalty Tribunal

JUDICIAL BRANCH

THE SUPREME COURT OF THE UNITED STATES

United States Courts of Appeals
United States District Courts
Territorial Courts
United States Court of International Trade
United States Court of Federal Claims
United States Court of Military Appeals
United States Tax Court
United States Court of Veterans Appeals
Administrative Office of the United States Courts
Federal Judicial Center
United States Sentencing Commission

EXECUTIVE BRANCH

THE PRESIDENT
Executive Office of the President

White House Office
Office of Management and Budget
Council of Economic Advisors
National Security Council

Office of the U.S. Trade Representative
Council on Environmental Quality
Office of Science and Technology Policy
Office of National Drug Control Policy

National Critical Materials Council
Office of Administration

THE VICE PRESIDENT

Department of Agriculture	Department of Commerce	Department of Defense	Department of Education	Department of Energy	Department of Health and Human Services	Department of Housing and Urban Development
Department of the Interior	Department of Justice	Department of Labor	Department of State	Department of Transportation	Department of the Treasury	Department of Veterans Affairs

INDEPENDENT ESTABLISHMENTS AND GOVERNMENT CORPORATIONS

ACTION
Administrative Conference of the U.S.
African Development Foundation
Central Intelligence Agency
Commission on Civil Rights
Commission on National and Community Service
Commodity Futures Trading Commission
Consumer Product Safety Commission
Defense Nuclear Facilities Safety Board
Environmental Protection Agency
Equal Employment Opportunity Commission
Export-Import Bank of the U.S.
Farm Credit Administration
Federal Communications Commission
Federal Deposit Insurance Corporation
Federal Election Commission

Federal Emergency Management Agency
Federal Housing Finance Board
Federal Labor Relations Authority
Federal Maritime Commission
Federal Mediation and Conciliation Service
Federal Mine Safety and Health Review Commission
Federal Reserve System
Federal Retirement Thrift Investment Board
Federal Trade Commission
General Service Administration
Inter-American Foundation
Interstate Commerce Commission
Merit Systems Protection Board
National Aeronautics and Space Administration
National Archives and Records Administration
National Capital Planning Commission

National Credit Union Administration
National Foundation on the Arts and the Humanities
National Labor Relations Board
National Mediation Board
National Railroad Passenger Corporation (Amtrak)
National Science Foundation
National Transportation Safety Board
Nuclear Regulatory Commission
Occupational Safety and Health Review Commission
Office of Government Ethics
Office of Personnel Management
Office of Special Counsel
Panama Canal Commission
Peace Corps
Pennsylvania Avenue Development Corporation
Pension Benefit Guaranty Corporation

Postal Rate Commission
Railroad Retirement Board
Resolution Trust Corporation
Securities and Exchange Commission
Selective Service System
Social Security Administration
Small Business Administration
Tennessee Valley Authority
Thrift Depositor Protection Oversight Board
Trade and Development Agency
U.S. Arms Control and Disarmament Agency
U.S. Information Agency
U.S. International Development Cooperation Agency
U.S. International Trade Commission
U.S. Postal Service

Powers, Checks, and Balances

Executive's relationship to legislative

✔ The president may recommend legislation (which must then be introduced by a member of the Senate or House).

✔ He can approve or veto legislation that has passed both houses of Congress.

✔ He can enter into treaties with foreign countries, and commit U.S. troops abroad.

✔ He also has the power to enforce the laws of the United States.

Executive's role with judicial

✔ The president appoints Supreme Court justices and other federal judges.

Judicial's role with executive

✔ The federal courts can review the constitutionality of executive branch actions.

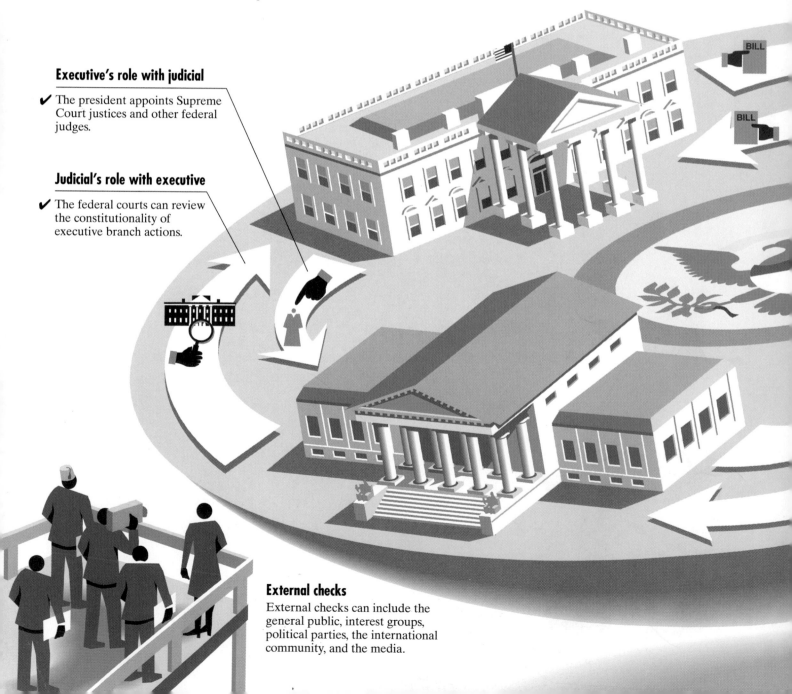

External checks

External checks can include the general public, interest groups, political parties, the international community, and the media.

Legislative's relationship to executive

- ✔ Congress may introduce and pass legislation.
- ✔ With a two-thirds vote of both houses Congress can override a presidential veto.
- ✔ The Senate must confirm the president's nominations for the Supreme Court, cabinet and certain other offices.
- ✔ Treaties entered into by the president must be ratified by Congress.
- ✔ Official declarations of war are made by Congress, who may refuse to appropriate funding for continued military actions initiated by the president.
- ✔ Congress oversees executive branch functions, and can impeach the president.

Judicial's role with legislative

- ✔ Federal courts can review the constitutionality of acts of Congress.

Legislative's role with judicial

- ✔ Congress establishes the courts (except for the Supreme Court, established by the Constitution) and their jurisdiction (the kinds of cases they can hear).
- ✔ Congress may overturn court decisions interpreting federal laws by passing new legislation.
- ✔ Congress has the authority to impeach judges.

THE EXECUTIVE BRANCH

CONTENTS

THE EXECUTIVE BRANCH is headed by the president of the United States. It is responsible for carrying out laws enacted by the president and Congress. In order to accomplish this mandate, the executive branch has evolved into an assortment of administrative, regulatory, and policy-implementing offices. Perhaps most notable of these offices are the 14 executive departments whose department heads are members of the president's cabinet. In addition to the cabinet, there are numerous agencies (the Central Intelligence Agency and Environmental Protection Agency, for example), committees, commissions (such as the Federal Trade Commission and Securities and Exchange Commission), and other offices that have been created by law or presidential directive and are also part of the executive branch. The members of the Executive Office and cabinet are the president's prime source of information. Together, they make up "the administration."

Many aspects of the executive branch will be discussed in greater detail throughout this section, but let's take a moment to briefly introduce some of them here.

The vice president is first in line to the Oval Office should the president be unable to fulfill his term. He serves as president of the Senate, although this is a primarily ceremonial role, and otherwise he has no real authority granted by the Constitution.

Within the Executive Office of the President are the White House Office, which is headed by the president's chief of staff, the Office of Management and Budget, the Council of Economic Advisors, the National Security Council, the Office of the U.S. Trade Representative, the Council on Environmental Quality, the Office of Science and Technology Policy, the Office of National Drug Control Policy, the National Critical Materials Council, the Office of the Vice President, and the Office of Administration.

The White House Office is headed by the president's chief of staff. This office both advises the president and acts as his representative in the areas of national security, economic affairs, and domestic policy matters.

The Office of Management and Budget (OMB) is the largest component of the executive branch. OMB assists the president in preparing the federal budget and determines the budgetary impact of all legislation that executive branch agencies submit to Congress.

The Council of Economic Advisors issues the president's annual economic report, which addresses issues such as employment, productivity, and buying power.

The authors of the Constitution were concerned about how much power and independence to give the executive branch. The result of their deliberations was a plan that called for a chief executive that would be chosen by electors every four years. His duties would include acting as commander-in-chief of the armed forces, ensuring that the laws were faithfully executed, and (subject to approval of the Senate) making appointments and treaties. The president would be required to work in conjunction with Congress; this requirement would keep the executive branch from assuming too much power and resembling the monarchy in England. Over time, strong presidents have enhanced their position by assuming certain powers that have been continued by their successors until those powers became, unofficially, part of the job. Additional power also results simply from the importance and prestige Americans associate with the office of president. Ready access to the media, combined with the public's willingness to listen, gives a president considerable power in garnering public support for his legislative proposals.

The president is directed by the Constitution to give a State of the Union address to Congress "from time to time." This has become an annual address in which the president presents his legislative agenda for the coming year before a joint session of Congress. In addition, the President presents an economic report that includes plans to maximize employment and a budget message that outlines spending and revenue proposals.

Despite how things appear in the organizational chart in Chapter 1, the president does not have total control of the executive branch. The size, structure, extent of authority, and financial resources are all overseen by Congress.

The Executive Office of the President plays a critical role in regulating the economy and protecting general welfare of our nation, but the actual running of the government is done by the many federal departments and agencies, often referred to as "the bureaucracy." Once the laws are enacted, it is the bureaucracy's primary function to implement them. Agencies within the bureaucracy acquire and maintain national parks, process Social Security claims, and monitor the safety of nuclear power plants, to mention just a few of their duties.

While the president does appoint agency heads, he cannot always count on their full support because they soon develop loyalties to their own agencies or departments. However, presidents and their advisors can gain some control through the budget process, serving as a central clearinghouse for executive branch legislative proposals and monitoring the implementation of legislation in departments and agencies.

The media play an active role in all branches of the federal government, but they may have the greatest impact on the executive branch. White House aides are constantly engaged in extensive public relations, and members of the media contend that presidents manipulate the public's understanding of issues (others may say that the media do this, too). Through their monitoring of every aspect of politics, however, the media attempt to provide a context in which the American people can consider statements, proposals, and actions of the executive branch.

CHAPTER 2

The President and Vice President

ONLY TWO GOVERNMENT officials are elected by the nation as a whole. They are our president and vice president. The president serves as both a political leader and a symbol of our nation and is the first thing many people think of when they consider the federal government. In turn, a president's most valuable asset is the support of the American people.

We expect great things from our president. Our criteria for judging the president are constantly changing, and his favorability rating will rise or fall with our perception of the nation's well-being. More than anyone else, the president has the daunting task of maintaining harmony among socioeconomic and racial groups, achieving economic growth and low unemployment, protecting the environment, and keeping peace. We want our president to be a leader who can pull all of us together, have a sense of vision, establish priorities, put forth a national agenda, cope with crises, and get things done. Perhaps most important, we expect our president to create a climate within which all of our diverse interests can function harmoniously together.

The Constitution specifies that the president serves as the nation's chief executive—with "executive power" to enforce the laws of the United States, issue executive orders, run the executive branch, and the like—and as commander-in-chief of the armed forces. With the Senate, he enters into treaties and appoints judges, ambassadors, and other high government officials. He alone has the authority to veto legislation proposed by Congress, while approval of legislation is shared with Congress as a whole.

In reality, a president's practical power and influence are generally enhanced in times of national crisis, if he wins the election by a large margin, or is ranked high in public opinion polls. If the American people are standing behind their chief executive, members of the legislative branch are far more likely to go along with his proposals. Conversely, presidential support is easily eroded by a low rating in the polls.

Presidential power can be constrained somewhat by less tangible limits. For example, his ability to weigh issues and select policy options is based upon the completeness and accuracy of the information presented to him. Special interest groups exert a great deal of pressure, both directly and through the media. The president's own realization that his decisions might have far-reaching effects on inflation, unemployment, or certain segments of the population can weigh heavily.

The first step in transforming campaign promises into workable programs or policies is to develop an agenda. Presidents may draw from campaign issues and promises, their own ideology, their party's platform, aides and campaign advisors, federal agencies, and outside experts. They will work hard to persuade Congress that their agenda should be the congressional agenda. The national press may publicize items already on the president's agenda or bring so much attention to a new issue that it, too, must be addressed.

There are considerable obstacles that make it nearly impossible for the president to enact sweeping reforms. No president starts with a blank slate. Along with attempting to deliver on campaign promises, he must cope with existing problems and programs. Not surprisingly, many national problems are far more complex than they appear, and rarely are there clear solutions. Government institutions are highly resistant to change (or elimination!). The president is not the only one with an agenda and must compete against other policy makers who have their own agendas, interests, and sources of power. This problem is probably at its most acute in the area of domestic policy because there are many competing interests—a proposal that is seen as beneficial by some is seen as outrageous by others.

A politically skillful president may be able to smooth over party differences and encourage Congress to go along with his agenda. The president influences Congress primarily through meetings with his party's leaders in the House and Senate and through his congressional liaison office. Occasionally, he may even call up a wavering member to discuss the issue personally.

Once presented with a bill that has passed both houses of Congress, the president has several options. He can sign the bill, or do nothing for ten working days, which will make it law. Or, he can exercise his power to veto the bill in one of two ways: First, he can veto the bill outright and send it back to Congress with his reasons for rejecting it. Second, should Congress adjourn before the president has signed a bill, it is effectively killed by pocket veto.

The second highest-ranking member of the executive branch is the vice president. The Constitution calls for the vice president to act as president, should that become necessary, and to serve as president of the senate. The vice president also serves as a member of the president's cabinet, by tradition, and of the National Security Council, by statute. Often, the president assigns his vice president various other political, executive, and ceremonial responsibilities that might include chairing a government commission or serving as goodwill ambassador abroad.

The Executive Office of the President is composed of numerous offices and councils, but we will review only the most prominent ones.

The White House Office consists of the key aides with whom the president has daily contact such as his chief of staff, press secretary, congressional liaisons, speech writers, and scheduler. Often these aides are a combination of people who have been drawn from the president's campaign staff, long-time associates in whom he has confidence, or experts in a specific field. The president's personal staff members are almost unfailingly loyal and are the first people he turns to for advice. They are responsible only to the president, and he can hire and fire them at will.

The president's chief of staff serves as his right hand and is the most visible White House aide. The chief of staff has instant access to the president and works very closely with him. The chief of staff may schedule the president's appointments, filter information that reaches the Oval Office, or serve as his spokesman before the media.

The Office of Management and Budget (OMB) is the largest component of the Executive Office. Perhaps the most well known function of OMB is preparing the president's annual budget. Because the budget determines which programs will get more funds, which will remain the same, and which will be cut, it can become a major vehicle for shaping the president's legislative priorities.

OMB studies the organization and operation of the executive branch, devises plans for reorganizing departments and agencies, and searches for ways to get better information about government programs.

OMB also serves as a clearinghouse for ideas before they are proposed to Congress. OMB staff members meticulously review major legislative proposals from the cabinet and other executive agencies, assess their budget implications, and then make recommendations to the president.

The staff of OMB is composed primarily of career officials who are traditionally nonpartisan in their evaluation of ongoing projects and new spending requests.

The National Security Council (NSC) was created to coordinate domestic, diplomatic, and military policies in matters of national security. This committee serves to link the president's key military and foreign policy advisors and has its own staff that prepares detailed analyses and presents policy options. Traditionally the president, the vice president, the secretaries of state and defense, and the director of the Central Intelligence Agency (CIA) are members of the council, but often the president will include other officials whose knowledge he considers to be especially relevant.

The Council of Economic Advisors makes recommendations to the president on economic issues, advises him on his economic policy, prepares the annual report of the Council of Economic Advisors, and helps the president form his policy on inflation, unemployment, and other economic matters.

Developing a Presidential Agenda

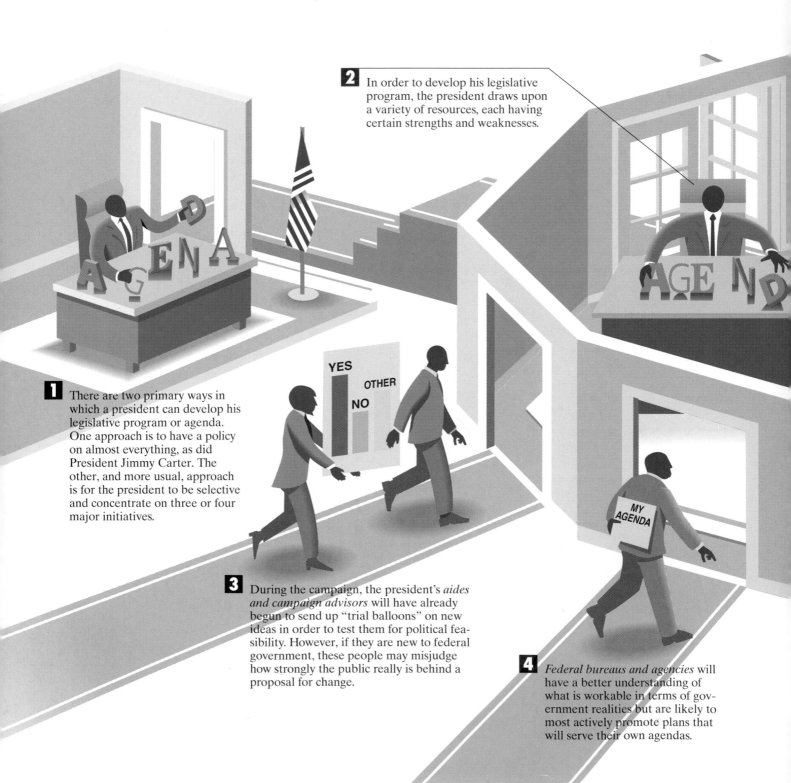

2 In order to develop his legislative program, the president draws upon a variety of resources, each having certain strengths and weaknesses.

1 There are two primary ways in which a president can develop his legislative program or agenda. One approach is to have a policy on almost everything, as did President Jimmy Carter. The other, and more usual, approach is for the president to be selective and concentrate on three or four major initiatives.

3 During the campaign, the president's *aides and campaign advisors* will have already begun to send up "trial balloons" on new ideas in order to test them for political feasibility. However, if they are new to federal government, these people may misjudge how strongly the public really is behind a proposal for change.

4 *Federal bureaus and agencies* will have a better understanding of what is workable in terms of government realities but are likely to most actively promote plans that will serve their own agendas.

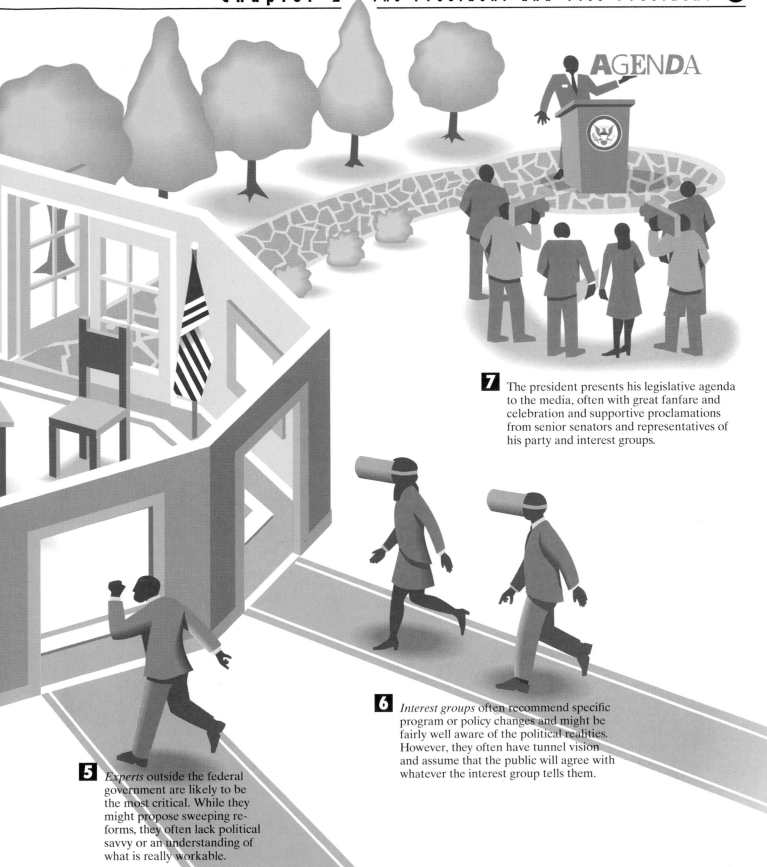

7 The president presents his legislative agenda to the media, often with great fanfare and celebration and supportive proclamations from senior senators and representatives of his party and interest groups.

6 *Interest groups* often recommend specific program or policy changes and might be fairly well aware of the political realities. However, they often have tunnel vision and assume that the public will agree with whatever the interest group tells them.

5 *Experts* outside the federal government are likely to be the most critical. While they might propose sweeping reforms, they often lack political savvy or an understanding of what is really workable.

Presidential Elections

MOST OF OUR presidents come to the White House after many years in the public arena. Since World War I, 80 percent of the major party candidates for president and vice president have served as either a state governor or U.S. senator. In addition to a history of public service and widespread name recognition, a serious candidate will have to be popular with voters. The speed with which information travels and the media's lust for scandal mean that "damage control" has become a primary aspect of today's presidential campaigns. Blunders are inevitable, and the candidate's ability to recover quickly and smoothly is essential.

Political parties play a key role in providing for the orderly transfer of power by acting as intermediaries between the public and the government. Parties provide alternative candidates and policies, and they help to educate the voters. They also help to ensure responsibility and accountability in government. Parties will be quick to point out the short-comings in the opposing parties' policies or leaders in hope of gaining credibility for their own candidates and programs.

In recent years, the public's mistrust of government and tendency to vote for the individual rather than along party lines (ticket splitting), and the decline in overall voter participation have contributed to the weakening of political parties. Real differences between Republicans and Democrats have blurred as parties try to appeal to the greatest number of voters. For example, environmental protection is no longer strictly the domain of Democrats, and Republicans are not alone in efforts to expand opportunities for U.S. businesses.

As the power of political parties has lessened, the power of interest groups has grown to fill the void. Party platforms are written to appeal to the widest possible range of voters in order to win elections, while interest groups focus on specific issues and thus can be perceived as better representing individual opinion on that issue. Perhaps for this reason, people often align themselves with a number of interest groups and the issues they champion, rather than with one or another political party.

The run for the White House is a lengthy, expensive, and carefully orchestrated process. Presidential hopefuls rely heavily on professional political consultants who can do everything from molding the candidate's image, developing a strategy, conducting polls, and handling campaign logistics, to advising candidates on their spouses' behavior or wardrobe.

Political consultants have moved into positions that were once held by party officials. Consultants bring expertise and savvy to a campaign and head up a team of campaign professionals—pollsters, media experts, staff—and volunteers who strive to convey the candidate's positions on the issues and convince voters that the candidate is honest, competent, and a real leader.

The focus of campaigns has always been to make contact with as many voters as possible. Once this was accomplished through rallies, parades, whistle-stop train tours, and shaking hands outside factory gates or in shopping center parking lots. Addressing small crowds still occurs to some degree because it appeals to voters as individuals, but candidates have increasingly devoted their energies and campaign funds to getting on television because television reaches more people than all of the other campaign methods put together.

Television coverage of candidates is not limited to paid political commercials, though commercials often contain a fair amount of information. Traditionally, commercials are geared toward voters who may not yet have made up their minds. The viewing public evaluates and remembers commercials, but it's often difficult to distinguish between fact and "humbug." Toward the end of a campaign, commercials often include responses to attacks from the opposition in an effort to get the "truth" out. The usual 30- or 60-second commercials may even be supplemented with longer, documentary-style presentations. Ross Perot's "infomercials" garnered a great deal of attention during the 1992 election. Many voters regarded these as entertainment and tuned in more to see what Perot would say next than because they intended to vote for him. In recent elections, call-in talk shows such as "Larry King Live" have been used with quite a bit of success by candidates to increase people's sense of involvement in the political process.

Voters often consider news coverage to be more credible than paid commercials, so campaign managers will notify the press whenever their candidate does something that might be considered newsworthy. The result is more likely to be a human-interest story than hard news. An incumbent president has a substantial advantage over challengers because he can make news by proposing new programs or taking credit for dramatic developments in international affairs.

Americans expect the leading presidential candidates to face off in televised debates that have been part of our election process since voters watched the Kennedy-Nixon debate in 1960. In recent elections, even the vice presidential nominees have participated in televised debates.

Despite questions of accuracy, the use of polls has become an important element in campaigns. While polls are thought to be readings of opinion, they can actually shape opinion by creating a bandwagon effect that carries along voters who want to be on the winning side. Polls can be a critical factor in fundraising. Contributors are unlikely to invest in a candidate behind in the polls because many feel that doing so is simply throwing money away.

The public's first official opportunity to voice their preference for a given candidate is in the state's caucus or primary election. The operation of caucuses and primaries varies from state to state. The New Hampshire primary and the Iowa caucus attract a great deal of media attention because they are held first, and (rightly or wrongly) they are seen as a good indication of the nation's choice for candidates. States have moved up the dates of their primaries, or joined regional primaries, in hopes of increasing their impact on establishing the ticket; later primaries are meaningless if they occur after many of the candidates have dropped out of the race and the front-runner's nomination is virtually assured. Party efforts to have regional primaries have resulted in the highly publicized Super Tuesday, a day when many states across the country now hold their primaries.

Roughly half as many people vote in primary as in general elections, and those who do participate in the primaries tend to be younger, more affluent, and better educated than the average voter in a general election.

The Democratic and Republican front-runners are generally established before the national convention takes place in midsummer. National conventions are a traditional fixture of presidential elections and retain some of the old-style political flavor, with demonstrations, marches, music, and behind-the-scenes negotiations in smoke-filled rooms. During the convention, parties nominate a presidential ticket and adopt a party platform. The selection of a vice presidential nominee who will balance the ticket often generates a great deal of speculation and excitement. Sometimes the choice is known before the convention, but usually this is not the case.

Party leaders do their best to put on a good show for the television audience, and peak viewing hours on both coasts are kept in mind when the schedule is drawn up. The highly partisan keynote speech, counting of ballots, and acceptance speeches of the vice presidential and presidential nominees all occur during prime time. Party unity and harmony are emphasized in a carnivallike atmosphere.

Ross Perot's third-party candidacy generated a great deal of attention in the 1992 election and contributed to a slightly higher than normal voter turnout. Traditionally, third party candidates offer more far-reaching solutions than major party candidates would ever dare to. Proposals for abolition of slavery, women's suffrage, social security, minimum wage, and the graduated income tax, for example, originated with third party candidates. What has often happened is that a major party has adopted a third party's platform, and, left without an issue, the third party has evaporated.

After the national conventions, the presidential campaign really gathers momentum, and it culminates in November when voters go to the polls. Our president is selected through a uniquely American institution known as the electoral college, but on election night a great deal of attention is focused on the popular vote.

The electoral college was created as a compromise between a direct popular vote and having Congress select the president. Despite calls for reform because of concern that the electoral vote does not necessarily represent the popular vote, we continue to use the system today.

The candidate who wins the popular vote in a state will win all of that state's electoral votes, and the candidate with the majority of electoral votes—270—becomes president. Because of this "winner take all" feature, candidates tend to concentrate on the larger states. Also, it is difficult for minor party candidates to compete under this system. Voters are often reluctant to "waste" their vote on a minor party candidate who cannot win the office.

One concern about using the electoral college to select a president is that it is possible for a candidate to win the popular vote and still lose the election. A candidate who wins the popular vote in a number of small states, but loses by a narrow margin in one or two of the big states might not have enough electoral votes to win the election despite having more popular votes.

The election is final when all the electoral votes are officially counted before a joint session of Congress. The new president is sworn in during a ceremony on the steps of the Capitol, and will then present his first speech as president to the American people.

The Electoral College

1 The census conducted every 10 years is used to determine, among other things, the number of congressional seats each state will have. Every state is allotted one electoral vote for each senator and representative. The electoral college consists of 538 electors—435 to cover the House of Representatives, 100 for the Senate, and 3 for the District of Columbia.

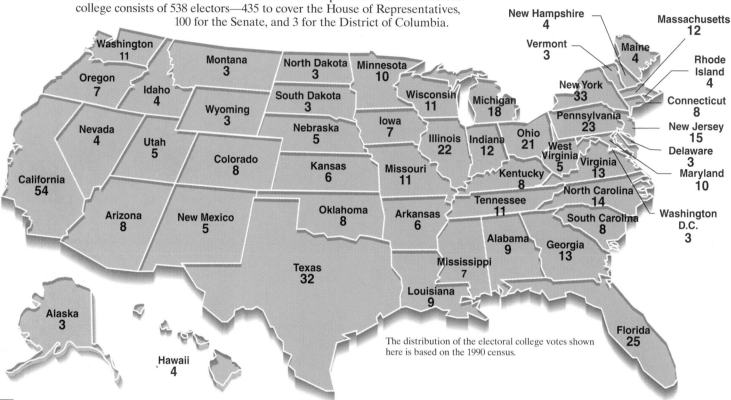

The distribution of the electoral college votes shown here is based on the 1990 census.

2 Parties in each state nominate electors. For example: Michigan has a total of 18 electoral votes. The Democrats and Republicans in Michigan each select 18 electors. In the event of an independent candidate, that candidate's party would also designate 18 electors. Electors may be state party leaders, selected by the state's party chairman or designated by state statute by virtue of their position. An elector may not be a member of Congress or hold any other federal office.

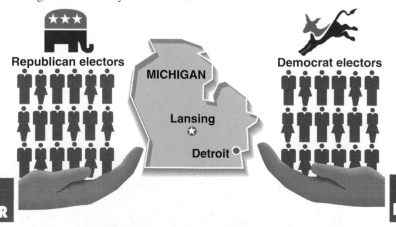

3 Every four years, on the Tuesday following the first Monday in November, Americans vote for their next president of the United States.

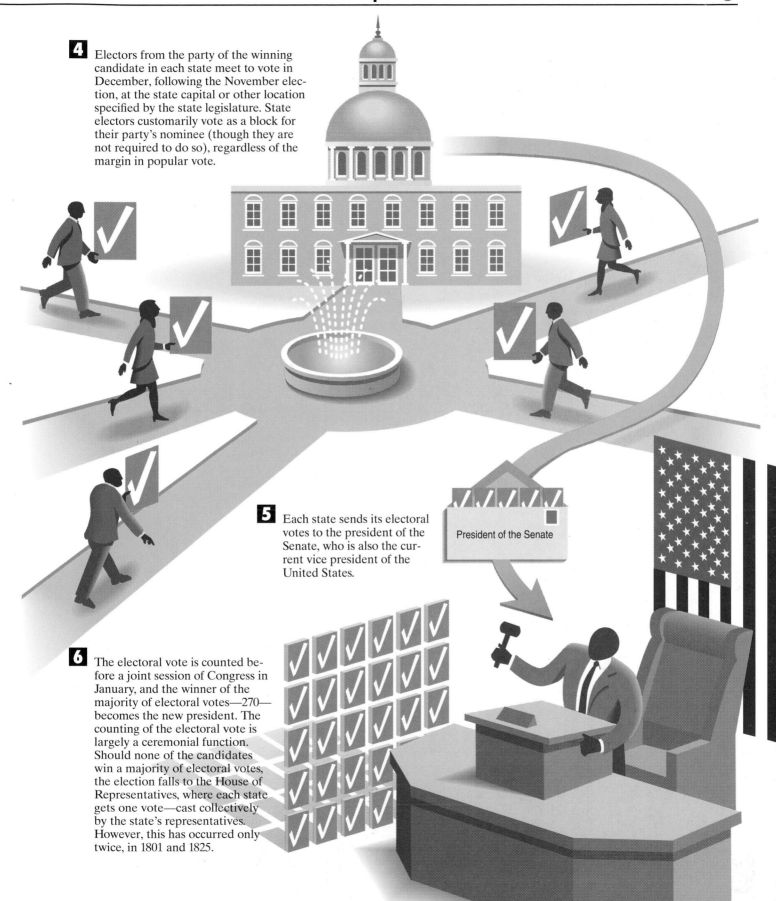

4 Electors from the party of the winning candidate in each state meet to vote in December, following the November election, at the state capital or other location specified by the state legislature. State electors customarily vote as a block for their party's nominee (though they are not required to do so), regardless of the margin in popular vote.

5 Each state sends its electoral votes to the president of the Senate, who is also the current vice president of the United States.

President of the Senate

6 The electoral vote is counted before a joint session of Congress in January, and the winner of the majority of electoral votes—270—becomes the new president. The counting of the electoral vote is largely a ceremonial function. Should none of the candidates win a majority of electoral votes, the election falls to the House of Representatives, where each state gets one vote—cast collectively by the state's representatives. However, this has occurred only twice, in 1801 and 1825.

The Line of Succession to the Oval Office

1 In the event that our president is unable to fulfill his duties, there is a clear line of succession to his office, shown in the illustration below. Despite this long list, no one other than the vice president has ever succeeded to the presidency.

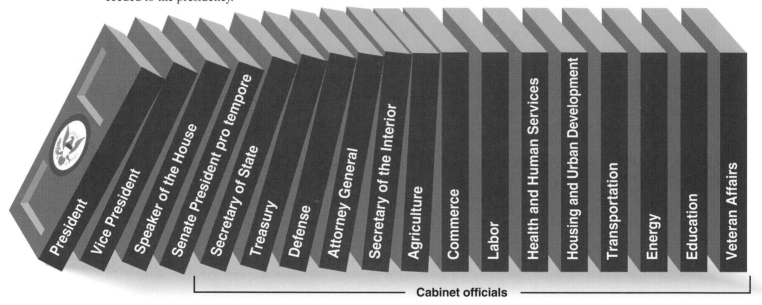

President · Vice President · Speaker of the House · Senate President pro tempore · Secretary of State · Treasury · Defense · Attorney General · Secretary of the Interior · Agriculture · Commerce · Labor · Health and Human Services · Housing and Urban Development · Transportation · Energy · Education · Veteran Affairs

Cabinet officials

3 Not until 1967, when the Twenty-fifth Amendment to the Constitution was ratified, did the United States have a clear system that provided for continuity in the White House in the event that the president became disabled. Prior to this, a vice president did not assume any presidential duties while an incapacitated president was still alive because it would appear as though he were trying to usurp the president's power. The Twenty-fifth Amendment provided a mechanism whereby a vice president could serve as the *acting* president in the event that the president were to become incapacitated.

2 Nine times in our history, the vice president has been sworn in as president. John Tyler, Millard Fillmore, Andrew Johnson, Chester Arthur, Theodore Roosevelt, Calvin Coolidge, Harry Truman, Lyndon Johnson, and Gerald Ford all were vice presidents who succeeded to the office of president.

John Tyler

Millard Fillmore

Andrew Johnson

Chester Authur

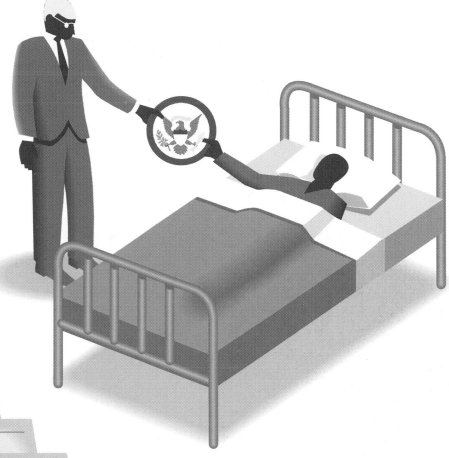

4 The vice president may serve as acting president in two situations. Should the president inform Congress that he is unable to carry out his duties, or in the event that he is incapable of making presidential decisions (as occurred when President Ronald Reagan was undergoing surgery after the assassination attempt), the vice president would become acting president until the president informed Congress that his disability had ended.

TIMES-POST

TIMES-POST

TIMES-POST

TIMES-POST

NIXON RESIGNS FORD TAKES OVER

5 When the office of vice president becomes vacant (by death, resignation, or succession to the presidency) the president nominates a vice president, who must then be confirmed by a majority vote in both houses of Congress. It is possible for the United States to have both a president and vice president who were not popularly elected. Neither Gerald Ford nor his vice president, Nelson Rockefeller, was elected. President Richard Nixon appointed Gerald Ford to replace his resigning vice president, Spiro Agnew. After Ford became president when Nixon resigned, he appointed Nelson Rockefeller to serve as his vice president.

Theodore Roosevelt

Calvin Coolidge

Harry Truman

Lyndon Johnson

Gerald Ford

The Cabinet

THE PRESIDENT'S CABINET consists of the heads of the 14 administrative departments of the executive branch, and any other officials that the President may include (for example, the ambassador to the United Nations is often asked to be a member). The 14 departments were created by acts of Congress, employ most of the federal government workers, and make up the bulk of what is commonly called the *bureaucracy*.

One of the first orders of business when a new president takes office is for him to nominate those who will head each agency and become his cabinet. Each nominee is subject to Senate approval.

Cabinet-level appointees come from a variety of backgrounds such as private industry, law, and education. Most have had some prior experience in working with the federal government. In selecting the nominees, a president will take into account a number of political considerations, trying to please powerful interest groups, address regional needs (for example, the secretary of the interior is often from a western state), and ensure that women and minorities are represented. Increasingly, the president has chosen individuals who are also known for expertise in areas related to a given department's jurisdiction.

Department heads are expected to be loyal to the administration even though they are often chosen for reasons other than their personal closeness to the president. While cabinet members would like to be able to cooperate with the president, they must first be responsive to the needs of their own agencies if they are going to be effective managers.

Department secretaries head vast organizations. They must oversee existing programs, address changing needs, and defend their budget requests. Of course, not every issue can be a top priority, and this leads to constant competition for limited resources. Departmental jurisdictions often overlap, and the departments involved may have conflicting agendas. For example, the competing needs of diplomacy versus military (the departments of State and Defense), labor versus business (the departments of Labor and Commerce), or urban versus rural (the departments of Housing and Urban Development, and Agriculture), and the need for funding (*all* departments) must be balanced against the need for fiscal restraint (the Office of Management and Budget). Because of the disparate functions and competing needs and agendas of each department, it is not feasible for the cabinet to function as a unified decision-making body.

While cabinet secretaries devote much of their energies to the "headline" issues, they rely heavily upon both their politically appointed staffs and career civil servants (whose expertise and skills are vital to the efficient functioning of the departments) in order to manage the agency's day-to-day business.

This "subcabinet" consists, in part, of under secretaries, assistant secretaries, commissioners, deputy assistant secretaries, general counsels, office directors, regional administrators, inspector generals, and their staffs. While the public is seldom aware of these officials, they head the many offices, agencies, and bureaus within the federal bureaucracy and can exert quite an influence on policy decisions by virtue of their position and expertise.

A great many career civil servants are highly educated professionals in fields such as engineering, applied and social sciences, economics, agriculture, and law. As we will see in the next chapter, government employees are more than mere "paper pushers." While many do, in fact, deal with great quantities of printed material, civil servants employed by the National Aeronautics and Space Administration (NASA), for example, have made it possible for man to walk on the moon and explore the farthest reaches of our universe!

The Cabinet at a Glance

Department of State, established in 1789. It advises the president on foreign policy, including treaty negotiations, and works to ensure the long-range security of the U.S.
- Annual Budget = $5,238,000,000
- Employees = 25,699

Department of Defense, established in 1947. DOD was formed when the formerly independent departments of the Army, Navy, and Air Force were consolidated. DOD manages the four separate military branches—Army, Navy, Air Force, and Marines—in order to ensure the security of our nation and deter war.
- Annual Budget = $305,508,000,000
- Employees = 1,012,716

Department of the Treasury, established in 1789. It serves as the government's banker, makes recommendations to the president on fiscal policy, manufactures our money, and collects taxes.
- Annual Budget = $303,023,000,000
- Employees = 166,433

Department of Health and Human Services (originally the Department of Health, Education, and Welfare), established in 1953. To protect our health and welfare, HHS oversees organizations such as the National Institutes of Health (NIH), the Centers for Disease Control and Prevention, and the Food and Drug Administration, as well as reimbursing states for money they spend on health care for the poor.
- Annual Budget = $292,695,000,000
- Employees = 129,483

Department of Labor, established in 1913, when it was separated from the Department of Commerce. Labor administers manpower programs and provides a variety of assistance to labor interests (such as supporting an increase in the minimum wage).
- Annual Budget = $17,938,000,000
- Employees = 43,343

Department of Housing and Urban Development, established in 1966. HUD is responsible for housing and urban programs. It insures mortgages, provides loans and subsidies for elderly, handicapped, and low income housing, and awards grants to cities for community development projects.
- Annual Budget = $25,573,000,000
- Employees = 14,998

Department of Justice, established in 1870. Headed by the U.S. attorney general, DOJ serves as the government's law firm. It protects the public from crime through law enforcement and prosecution of offenders and enforces drug, immigration, and naturalization laws.

- Annual Budget
  = $10,519,000,000
- Employees = 90,821

Department of Energy, established in 1977. DOE governs every aspect of the nation's energy policy, including nuclear power, researches current and alternative sources, and advises the president on the nation's energy policy.
- Annual Budget
  = $16,859,000,000
- Employees = 19,539

Department of Agriculture, established in 1862. It inspects food and administers farm subsidy, crop insurance, soil and water conservation, and food stamp programs. The National School Lunch Program is within its jurisdiction.
- Annual Budget
  = $67,169,000,000
- Employees = 125,640

Department of Commerce, established in 1903. Commerce conducts the U.S. census, provides economic and social statistics, and aides business by promoting trade and economic growth. It was originally the Department of Commerce and Labor.
- Annual Budget
  = $3,061,000,000
- Employees = 38,087

Department of Transportation, established in 1966. DOT oversees federal highway programs and mass transit. The Federal Aviation Administration, Federal Highway Administration, and the U.S. Coast Guard are all within its jurisdiction.
- Annual Budget
  = $35,913,000,000
- Employees = 69,831

Department of the Interior, established in 1849. Interior manages the nation's natural resources, including public lands and wildlife; conducts conservation and reclamation programs; and manages hydroelectric power.
- Annual Budget
  = $7,155,000,000
- Employees = 81,683

Department of Education, established in 1979 when it was separated from HHS. It administers U.S. education programs and awards funding to local school systems. Gallaudet University (for hearing-impaired students), Howard University (open to all, but emphasizing higher education for black students), and the printing of Braille books are within its jurisdiction.

- Annual Budget
  = $30,880,000,000
- Employees = 5,081

Department of Veterans Affairs, established in 1988. Takes care of the needs of veterans and their survivors, maintains VA hospitals, and offers benefits such as low interest loans for education and housing.
- Annual Budget
  = $35,361,000,000
- Employees = 256,145

* Employment and budget figures are from The U.S. Department of Commerce's *Statistical Abstract of the United States, 1993.* Employment figures are for civilian employees as of 1991. Budget outlays are 1993 estimates.

Elevating the Veterans Administration to a Cabinet-Level Department

During the 100th Congress, the Veterans Administration was awarded cabinet status. While the idea of granting a chair in cabinet meetings to veterans was not a new one, President Ronald Reagan's endorsement, combined with changing demographics, virtually ensured that the time had come.

The VA oversees a vast health care system of hospitals, nursing homes, and outpatient clinics, in addition to cemeteries and regional offices all around the country.

In the late 1980s, millions of World War II veterans (and their spouses) were reaching an age where they would be needing more of the services and benefits provided by the VA.

The president's campaign against government expansion was not undermined because granting the VA cabinet status was not going to increase its size or cost much money.

Veterans groups lobbied strongly for a change in status, arguing that
the VA was too big an agency, overseeing too many programs, not to be
included in cabinet meetings—especially during budget negotiations.

Opponents argued that veterans already had too much power, that
granting them a cabinet post would make them too influential in the
budgetary process, and that members of Congress were afraid to say
no to such a large number of voters.

To guarantee that the bill awarding cabinet status to veterans would be passed before
the 100th Congress adjourned, provisions requiring an overhaul of the VA's accounting
system were added, and controversial provisions (for example, allowing veterans to
appeal adverse rulings on benefits in court and establishing a governmental commission
to study the effectiveness of cabinet-style government) were removed.

CHAPTER 5

The Bureaucracy

THE BUREAUCRACY, considered part of the executive branch, is by far the largest part of the federal government. Included within the bureaucracy are a variety of departments, offices, agencies, and commissions, each with its own interests, agendas, and way of doing things.

While elected officials may come and go, the bureaucrats who carry out the day-to-day business of government remain in office. The work done by career civil servants is similar to that done by workers throughout the private sector. Only a small percentage of the professionals, clerks, computer operators, and maintenance workers who make up the federal bureaucracy work in the nation's capital. Most are employed in federal offices throughout the country.

Unlike in the private sector, however, it is rare for civil servants to be fired—even when they are poor performers or no longer needed. The process that must be followed in order to demote or suspend a civil servant is complicated and lengthy, and therefore rarely undertaken by supervisors.

Federal employees can, however, lose their jobs as a result of budget cuts. This firing process is known as "reduction in force." Not surprisingly, job security is heavily dependent on avoiding budget cuts. Bureaucrats sometimes expend tremendous effort on justifying their program's existence, protecting their agency's budget, and hiding any unfavorable data. Sometimes, carrying out the agency's mission becomes secondary to justifying its existence.

Bureaucrats do not just carry out the policies developed by Congress and the president, they also contribute to shaping them. Policies are typically written in rather general terms that acquire more precise meaning when they are applied to real-life situations. Therefore, those who implement policy must interpret its meaning—sometimes with the help of the courts. When problems are discovered, bureaucrats are in the most advantageous position to make suggestions for change and improvements. These suggestions may even become the basis for future administrative action and legislation.

The federal bureaucracy touches our daily lives in countless ways. While we may complain at great length about the bureaucracy, or civil servants, many of the tasks performed by the government are vital to the public interest. While private industry has moved into some areas that were once exclusively the government's territory (the delivery of parcels and express mail, for example), the government has far more extensive resources (taxes) than any one corporation, and it can provide programs that promote the security and well-being of individuals without being concerned about profit.

In order to convey a sense of the breadth and scope of the federal bureaucracy, let's look at some of the parts and what they do.

United States business and labor interests are enhanced by agencies such as the Bureau of Labor Statistics, within the Department of Labor, and the Small Business Administration (SBA). The Bureau of Labor Statistics monitors and distributes a variety of data concerning workers, workplace health and safety, productivity, pricing, and consumer buying. It strives to provide data that are impartial and of consistently high quality in an effort to accurately portray our rapidly changing economy. The SBA enhances opportunities for small businesses by making loans, providing counseling, and ensuring that small businesses are awarded their share of the government "pie."

Despite technological advances that make it possible to carry out our day-to-day affairs without ever actually touching money, most of us still have a need for cash. Coins are provided by the U.S. Mint. The Bureau of Engraving and Printing designs and manufactures our paper currency, postage stamps, and items such as Federal Reserve notes and Treasury securities.

In banking, the Federal Reserve System contributes to the strength of the U.S. economy by ensuring the soundness of the banking industry through policy-making and regulation. Our money supply is protected through insurance coverage on bank deposits provided by the Federal Deposit Insurance Corporation (FDIC).

The only federal agency whose employees can engage in collective bargaining is the U.S. Postal Service. Nearly 700,000 employees are required to deliver roughly 166 billion pieces of mail each year.

Working in close conjunction with state and local governments, the Federal Emergency Management Agency (FEMA) plans, prepares for, and responds to emergencies such as earthquakes, hurricanes, or floods.

The Nuclear Regulatory Commission (NRC) licenses and inspects our nuclear facilities and oversees the safe handling and disposal of radioactive materials.

Members of the Foreign Service (within the Department of State) report to the president and secretary of state on developments abroad that may influence the security and well-being of Americans. This information is often used in formulating our foreign policy.

Peace Corps volunteers work to promote goodwill worldwide by providing expertise and training programs for people in poor and undeveloped countries.

The nation's oldest federal law enforcement agency is the U.S. Marshalls Service, established in 1789. U.S. Marshalls provide security for federal courts, judges, and jurors; arrest federal fugitives; operate the federal witness protection program; and confiscate and sell property forfeited to the government. Marshalls may also be called to assist during times of civil unrest.

The Federal Bureau of Investigation (FBI), Central Intelligence Agency (CIA), and Drug Enforcement Administration (DEA) conduct a variety of investigative and law enforcement activities. The FBI concentrates its efforts on organized crime, drugs, counterterrorism, and white-collar and violent crimes. The CIA works to safeguard national security by collecting, assessing, and circulating information on developments around the world. The CIA advises the National Security Council, operate counterintelligence, and handle special projects for the president. The DEA heads the charge in our nation's fight against drugs through its enforcement of laws regarding controlled substances. The DEA concentrates on high-level drug smuggling and distribution schemes, both within the United States and abroad. They also administer regulations pertaining to the legal manufacture, distribution, and sale of controlled substances.

Transportation safety is enhanced by a variety of offices within the Department of Transportation. Among them are the National Transportation Safety Board (NTSB), which investigates accidents involving aircraft, railroads, pipelines, and highways; the Federal Aviation Administration (FAA), which controls U.S. airspace for both civilians and the military by regulating air traffic; and the National Highway Traffic Safety Administration (NHTSA). The FAA operates air traffic control towers, sets minimum standards for the manufacture and maintenance of aircraft, and addresses related issues such as aircraft noise in residential areas. The NHTSA was established in an effort to reduce the number of deaths and injuries resulting from motor vehicle accidents on the nation's highways. It provides information on the likelihood of car damage in the event of an accident and on the ease of repair after an accident, protects those who have purchased vehicles with altered odometers, ensures that guidelines for establishing speed limits are applied uniformly nationwide, and sets fuel economy standards.

While the descriptions of these bureaucratic offices and functions are brief, please keep in mind that the federal bureaucracy extends far beyond what can be covered in this short chapter!

Natural Resources and the Environment

The Environmental Protection Agency (EPA) coordinates federal and state efforts to protect the environment. EPA has established minimum standards for soil, water, and air quality and enforces compliance of businesses and local governments. The EPA manages the Superfund, a program that was developed to clean up the nation's hazardous waste sites, administers "Community Right To Know" programs that enable the public to find out about hazardous waste produced or situated near homes, controls toxic substances, and establishes tolerances for pesticide residues in food.

Within the Department of Justice, the Environmental and Natural Resources Division serves as the nation's legal advisor on environmental issues. They address topics such as the protection of endangered habitats and species, global warming, acquisition of federal property, Native American rights, and hazardous waste site remediation.

Natural Resources and the Environment

The following are among the government agencies that oversee our public lands: The National Park Service maintains our national monuments and parks and administers such programs as the National Register of Historic Places, the National Wild and Scenic Rivers System, and the Smithsonian Institution. The Bureau of Land Management oversees more than 270 million acres of land (including such natural resources as timber and minerals), leases grazing rights, and maintains records of mining claims. The National Forest Service works to ensure sustainable use of our forests and oversees recreational activities such as fishing and hunting.

The U.S. Fish and Wildlife Service works to conserve, protect, and enhance the natural habitats of fish, game, and migratory birds. The service conducts environmental impact assessments for hydroelectric dams and nuclear power sites and works with states to improve conservation efforts.

The Soil Conservation Service assists developers, land owners, farmers, and community planners with soil conservation and pollution control.

Worker and Consumer Protection

The Occupational Safety and Health Review Commission administers OSHA (the Occupational Safety and Health Act of 1970) by working to reduce job-related illnesses, injuries, and deaths. Under OSHA, employers are required to provide a safe workplace. Safety and health inspections are performed by the commission to ensure compliance.

The Job Training Partnership Act, under the Department of Labor, was established to place people for whom it is extraordinarily difficult to find employment (dislocated workers and economically disadvantaged young people, for example) in permanent, private-sector jobs.

Worker and Consumer Protection

The Consumer Product Safety Commission strives to protect the public from product-related illness, injury, or death. They establish uniform safety standards, evaluate the safety of products, conduct research, and investigate accidents.

The Equal Employment Opportunity Commission (EEOC) works to eliminate discrimination in all areas of employment. It investigates alleged discrimination and attempts to remedy the situation when discrimination has taken place.

The National Labor Relations Board (NLRB) administers labor law, works to prevent unfair labor practices, and protects the right of employees to organize into unions and bargain collectively.

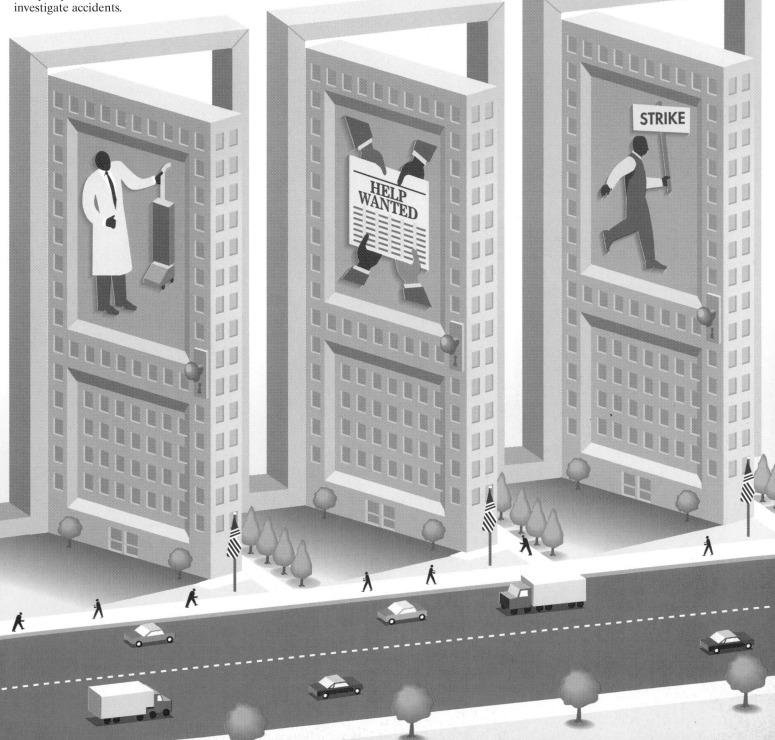

Bureaucratic 'Uglies' and Some Reasons They Exist

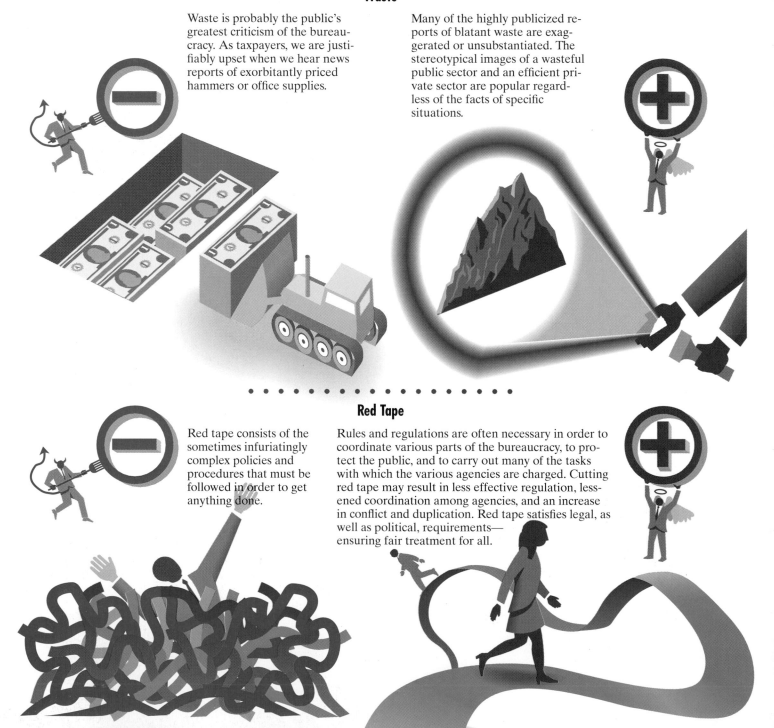

Waste

Waste is probably the public's greatest criticism of the bureaucracy. As taxpayers, we are justifiably upset when we hear news reports of exorbitantly priced hammers or office supplies.

Many of the highly publicized reports of blatant waste are exaggerated or unsubstantiated. The stereotypical images of a wasteful public sector and an efficient private sector are popular regardless of the facts of specific situations.

Red Tape

Red tape consists of the sometimes infuriatingly complex policies and procedures that must be followed in order to get anything done.

Rules and regulations are often necessary in order to coordinate various parts of the bureaucracy, to protect the public, and to carry out many of the tasks with which the various agencies are charged. Cutting red tape may result in less effective regulation, lessened coordination among agencies, and an increase in conflict and duplication. Red tape satisfies legal, as well as political, requirements—ensuring fair treatment for all.

Conflict and Duplication

Conflict results when agencies are working at cross-purposes to one another. Duplication of effort results when more than one agency is tasked with doing the same thing.

Congress has learned that it is far easier to add a new program than to cut an existing one—regardless of whether or not that program is in conflict with existing programs. In this way they can satisfy those requesting action without short-changing those whose needs have already been addressed through another program.

Growth

Growth, or imperialism, is the tendency government agencies have to grow, irrespective of their importance or usefulness.

The increase in federal bureaucracy is small when compared to the growth of the U.S. population and budget. However, employment of federal contractors and consultants (not technically bureaucrats) has mushroomed in recent years. Furthermore, it is far easier to add programs or offices than to cut them. This can often lead to redundancy and the existence of programs that have outlived their usefulness or are in conflict with other programs.

The President and the Media

THE MEDIA, especially television, play a critical role in our political system. They provide information that enables the public to evaluate the issues, elected officials, and the performance of government as a whole. Through their unique position, the media can influence what issues get national attention (and for how long), make or break political careers, and uncover incidents of wrong-doing.

The president and members of the media each have something the other needs. The president needs the media to enhance his visibility and promote his successes in order to foster continued public support, while the media need access to the president and information on his activities in order to meet their audience's demands.

While the media may try to present their views as though they were impartial, the media frequently take on an adversarial role. In fact, regardless of the party in power, their portrayal of the president tends to be negative. Few Americans think the media are entirely unbiased. While the media are often referred to as though they were a single entity, in reality they are far from monolithic, representing a wide range of philosophy and opinion. For example, while studies have often shown the press to be relatively "liberal," the majority of currently influential radio talk-show commentators are quite conservative.

Rarely does an individual ascend to the office of president without having gained considerable skill in handling journalists. And, although the president is the focus of scrutiny and criticism, he is also in a unique position to "make" the news. Through the use of staged events such as press conferences, photo opportunities, briefings, and ceremonies, the president—and to a lesser degree other media-savvy politicians—can use the media to create national priorities and rally public support. Planned "leaks" of information are another common way for those in power to manipulate the press.

While the frequency of presidential press conferences has declined somewhat in recent years, they remain a powerful tool for an incumbent president for several reasons. In this format, the media's role as an intermediary is virtually nonexistent. Presidents are often well prepared to side-step any questions and shape their answers in ways that will offend the fewest numbers of people.

Television networks typically cover the event "live," thus giving the president an opportunity to directly address the viewers at home. Often a press conference will be announced to respond to a politically volatile issue, but the president will instead use most of the allotted time to focus on other, more positive, items on his agenda. Attesting to the value of press conferences is the fact that a president will frequently experience an upward jump in his popularity rating immediately afterward.

Television news has both strengths and weaknesses. Constraints inherent in the medium of television greatly effect what aspects of the presidency are covered. By necessity, news reports must be short and uncomplicated. Stories that lend themselves to interesting film clips are more likely to be aired. For example, the ceremony of the signing of a bill makes for a snappier visual image than does negotiating an agreement. A relatively minor event may get coverage simply because it fits nicely with an ongoing story.

Because television news is both concise and easy to understand, it enjoys a substantial audience. However, many viewers who have gotten used to seeing complex issues in such a simplified form may believe that they are getting the whole story when, in fact, all they have really been exposed to are "headlines." People who want more in-depth information often choose alternative sources such as newspapers, news magazines, or public radio.

The growth of nationally popular call-in programs such as "Rush Limbaugh" on radio and "Larry King Live" on television, as well as countless local talk-radio programs, has been phenomenal in recent years. According to a May 1993 study by the Times Mirror Center for the People and the Press, nearly one-half of all Americans listen to talk radio (one in six listens regularly). This audience tends to be more conservative, more anti-Congress, and more likely to participate in the political process by attending public meetings, writing letters to elected officials, and voting.

The broad protections afforded by the First Amendment give the press tremendous freedom in deciding what issues are worth covering, policing the performance of government, and telling the public just what they should consider important. Our level of confidence in what the media tell us varies. College graduates, business professionals, and those in higher income brackets tend to place more trust in newspapers than they do in television, while younger Americans, the less educated, and lower-income individuals tend to be fairly confident that what they hear on television is truthful. These individuals are less likely to look to other sources, such as newspapers, for more in-depth information.

The relationship between presidential candidates, the media, and the public is somewhat circular. Candidates rely on the media to make voters aware of their candidacies. The media rely on candidates to provide them with newsworthy material that will interest their audience, the public. Voters find it easy to rely on newspapers, radio, and television as their principle sources of information on presidential candidates because of the flood of political reporting.

First used during the 1960 presidential campaign, televised debates are now an integral part of our presidential election season. During a debate, candidates present their views in response to questions posed by the media and remarks made by their opponents. The real effect of debates on voters can be hard to determine. Viewers are often more impressed by style than substance. For example, radio listeners expressed the view that Richard Nixon won his first debate with John Kennedy, but those who saw the debate on television believed just the opposite. The barrage of media commentary and speculation immediately following a debate tends to magnify certain aspects and exclude others. News coverage can enhance a victory, or emphasize a loss, through constant repetition of short excerpts. Voters who rely on the media to tell them the highlights of a debate may get an entirely different picture than if they had actually watched and listened to it themselves.

The powerful hold incumbent presidents have on the media's attention gives them a tremendous advantage when running for reelection. Yet, as has been noted, the president is often the object of intensely negative media coverage. The relationship between the president and the media, and the implications of it, are extremely complex.

How the Media Can Influence Public Policy

The lead story on the network news or a front-page headline attracts the public's attention and is prominently positioned so that viewers know it is an issue the media believe is important. Even a single news story can create a ripple effect. If members of the public with related concerns come forward, additional stories may be done and even more attention will be brought to an issue.

The media publicize issues that are already on the national agenda, and they help to put new items on the agenda by drawing attention to problems for which individuals and groups may seek legislative solutions. Often the media will keep an issue alive, and the public's attention focused, until some government action has been taken.

If the government does not respond, the media, through constant and intense coverage of an issue, can create an environment in which the public demands that their elected officials take action. Pressure exerted by the media can be beneficial when it pushes the government forward, or detrimental if elected officials respond with haphazard decision-making.

Media attention can both promote and impede political decision-making. The media's emphasis on dramatic events helps to keep an issue alive but can also compress the time elected officials have available to address problems and develop programs. Long-term planning does not always fit easily into the television mind-set.

Same-day television coverage of the Vietnam War and the vivid images of American military personnel wounded and killed in action were unprecedented. Beginning with this era, the media served to intensify the public's scrutiny and criticism of government policy.

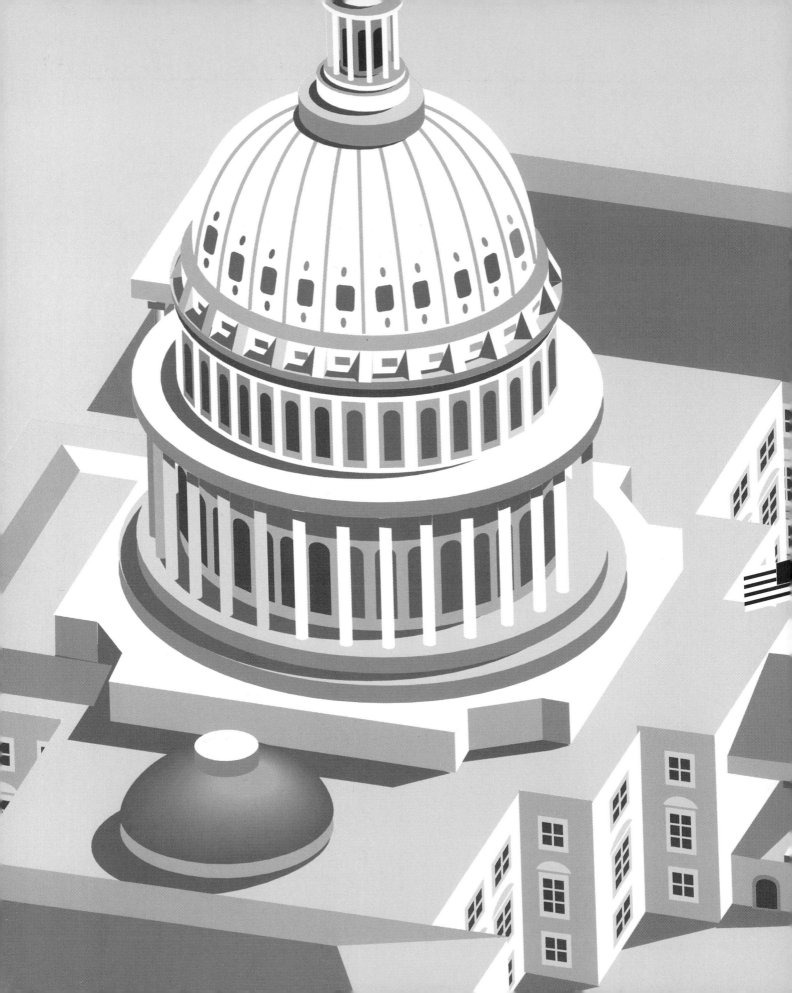

THE LEGISLATIVE BRANCH

CONTENTS

CONGRESS DOMINATES the legislative branch of our government and is charged with representing the people, making laws, and overseeing federal government operations. Two equally powerful bodies, the Senate and the House of Representatives, make up the Congress, and each chamber has its own procedures and customs. With 435 members, the House must adhere to a fairly rigid leadership and procedural structure to maintain some semblance of order, while the Senate, with only 100 members, is able to conduct its business with less formality and can even choose to disregard its own rules altogether.

While the authors of the Constitution were somewhat vague in their description of tasks for the president, this was not the case for Congress. Powers granted to the legislative branch include the ability to tax, borrow money, provide for a monetary system, regulate commerce, establish lower federal courts, maintain a military, and declare war. The Constitution implies powers that are not expressly granted in the famous "necessary and proper" clause that enables Congress to respond to any unforeseen needs. This rather vague mandate gives Congress a great deal of latitude in deciding when and how to legislate and has provided the basis for a vast expansion of congressional power.

Perhaps most important of all Congress's powers is the ability to impose taxes and allocate money—the "power of the purse." *Taxing* enables Congress to raise the revenues needed for running the country, and *spending* puts Congress in a position to determine policy on nearly every aspect of our daily lives. In fact, Congress spends most of its time on work related to the raising and spending of revenues.

Almost as important as the ability to tax and spend is the power to regulate commerce, for this puts Congress in a position to oversee the manufacture, transport, sale, and even safety of many products and services.

Congress is also charged with providing for "general welfare of the United States." Under this heading have come a variety of public assistance programs such as Social Security, unemployment and disability insurance, agricultural subsidies, food stamps, and Medicare and Medicaid.

While it may seem as though Congress has free rein to do as it pleases, it is significantly limited by the First Amendment, which states that "Congress shall make no law respecting an establishment of religion, or prohibiting the free exercise thereof; or abridging the freedom of speech, or of the press; or the right of the people peaceably to assemble, and to petition the Government for a redress of grievances." Further limitations on Congress result from the Fifth Amendment, which guarantees that Americans cannot "be deprived of life, liberty, or property, without due process of law; nor shall private property be taken for public use, without just compensation."

The powers of Congress are considerable, but in order to pass laws, Congress and the president must cooperate with one another—regardless of which party is in control of the White House, Senate, or Congress. The president is in an unparalleled position not only to establish an agenda but also to guide public opinion. Therefore, it is not unusual for Congress to consider topics that the president has put on the national agenda.

The power to declare war was granted to Congress in the Constitution. However, nuclear proliferation (and the fact that sizable military actions occur that are never officially declared "wars") has made this power somewhat obsolete. Congress's deliberative methods do not readily lend themselves to making the immediate decisions necessary now that communications are sent electronically and armies travel by air, instead of on foot. Therefore, the decision of whether to commit U.S. troops abroad has shifted to the president, who was granted the authority to deploy troops by the War Powers Act of 1973. Even Congress's power of the purse does not give Congress tremendous control over military intervention. Once the president has committed U.S. troops, it is very difficult for Congress to call a halt to military action.

Because members of Congress are elected to serve the needs of their constituents (the basis for our representative government), they devote considerable staff and resources to bringing federal dollars back to their districts (often referred to as "pork") and helping their constituents resolve any problems they have in dealing with the federal bureaucracy. Members who are not attuned to their constituents' needs or who don't deliver on their promises may not be reelected. This fact helps to ensure that those in office stay in touch with the people who sent them to Washington.

In order to carry out its daily business, Congress relies heavily upon its staff and the considerable information resources and staff expertise provided by the Library of Congress, General Accounting Office, and Congressional Budget Office. (These congressional support agencies, in addition to others, are discussed in greater detail in Chapter 8.)

Lobbyists and interest groups play an increasingly active role in our legislative process. Growth in the number of lobbyists has paralleled the expansion of federal government into new areas and the increase in federal spending. Because the supply of federal dollars is not unlimited, these groups must compete with one another in order to ensure that spending in their area of interest will be maintained, or perhaps even expanded.

Congressional ethics have attracted a great deal of attention in recent years, and the allegations against members of Congress for their involvement in illegal or immoral activities seem to be increasing at an alarming rate—much to the consternation of voters.

The Senate and the House of Representatives

MEMBERS OF THE Senate and the House of Representatives have a number of critical roles. They must legislate, serve their constituents, and oversee many aspects of government operations. And, if they want to continue to serve, they must run for reelection.

Legislating requires members to study issues; consult with experts, staff, and colleagues; attend meetings of sub- and full committees; follow and perhaps participate in floor debates; and vote in a way that best represents the needs of their constituents and party.

The lack of national consensus on issues is reflected in Congress. Major questions are often left unresolved for years as compromises are drafted, and redrafted, and both sides scramble for the votes needed for passage or rejection. Frequently, difficult decisions are put off until the final hour, and the last month of a session becomes a blinding whirl of legislative activity and late-night meetings.

Constituent service demands a considerable portion of a member's staff and time. Included in serving the voters are meeting with constituents, helping to solve problems they have with the federal government, responding to their letters and phone calls, delivering speeches, and working with interest groups to pass legislation of benefit to them.

House members, especially, are constantly concerned with the next election (every other year). Most return to their districts nearly every weekend to keep in close contact with their constituents, maintain visibility and accessibility, and—they hope—win reelection. Senators have a more relaxed election schedule (every six years), but they still must keep up relations with the voters who put them in office.

Congress can also serve as a forum for public policy. Congressional hearings on issues that affect a large segment of the population (Social Security and welfare, for example) or are hot topics in the news (gun control and medical waste disposal) may attract the attention of the public. The Iran-Contra and Watergate hearings serve as examples of how, in unusual cases, congressional hearings spark a great deal of public interest and encourage scrutiny of government. Legislators may take advantage of media attention to address contemporary issues, and the remarks of members (especially Senators) appeal to wide audiences.

Most of the work of Congress takes place in committees. These are specialized groups that enable Congress to address the wide range of issues that come before it. Committees are the key policy-making bodies in Congress and are used to select from the thousands of bills submitted those that will receive serious attention and perhaps eventual floor consideration.

In addition to standing (permanent) committees, each committee is broken down into subcommittees. There are also special and select committees that typically have a finite purpose and duration. The Senate Select Committee on Ethics, for example, meets when necessary to investigate alleged ethics violations of senators. The House Special Committee on Aging reviewed issues of importance to the elderly until it, along with other special House committees, was dispanded in 1993 as part of efforts to reduce the federal budget deficit.

Committees also have legislative oversight—the process of monitoring the bureaucracy and its administration of policy. Legislative oversight occurs mainly through hearings, and each committee is charged by law with monitoring the activities of the departments and agencies that come under its jurisdiction. In reality, Congress can oversee only a small fraction of bureaucratic activity because of the vastness of the federal bureaucracy and limitations of time and resources.

The Speaker of the House presides over the House of Representatives and is typically a senior member of the majority party. Not all speakers are equally powerful, and throughout our history, power in the House has shifted among strong speakers and powerful committee chairmen. However, the Speaker of the House is by far the most influential member of Congress. The Speaker's duties are not specified in the Constitution but, like many aspects of our government, have evolved over time. Much of the time the Speaker does not preside over floor debates, but instead delegates that role to another party member. Generally, the Speaker will take the chair when matters that he considers to be especially important are before the House. The Speaker typically exercises considerable control over the question of which bills are assigned to what committee and can regulate floor debate by granting members the right to speak. Avid C-SPAN viewers may have noticed that time limits are not always strictly adhered to during debates and that votes on important or controversial bills are held open so that late members can make it to the floor, so that the leadership can encourage members to change their votes in order to ensure a victory when the margin is tight.

There is no position in the Senate comparable to the House's Speaker. The Constitution names the vice president as president of the Senate and authorizes the vice president to vote in the event of a tie. In reality, the vice president rarely presides over the Senate chamber. The senior senator of the majority party is typically appointed president pro tempore (meaning, *for the time being*) to preside when the vice president is not present. While the president pro tempore presides over floor debates, the Senate has granted relatively little authority to this position.

Caucuses are organizations of party members in each chamber. At the beginning of each two-year term, caucuses vote to select their top leaders. These newly elected leaders then make several key appointments (committee chairs, for example), which must be approved by the party caucus, in order to complete their party's leadership structure. In addition to party caucuses, there are special caucuses. These organizations allow members to pursue interests important to them and their constituents. Examples of special caucuses include the Republican Study Committee and Democratic Study Group, the Northeast-Midwest Congressional Coalition, the Congressional Black Caucus, the Caucus on Women's Issues, and the Travel and Tourism Caucus.

A combined meeting of the House and Senate is called a joint session of Congress. Joint sessions are held in the larger House chamber and may be called for a presidential address or if a foreign leader is invited to speak before Congress. The Constitution requires Congress to meet jointly every four years to count the electoral votes for president and vice president.

Two of the most powerful employees of Congress are the parliamentarians for the Senate and House. Their interpretation of rules and precedents can have a profound impact on the course of floor action and the eventual shape of legislation. Parliamentarians do not actually make rulings, but it is rare for a presiding officer to ignore their advice.

The Senate

House

Senate

1 The Senate is made up of 100 members, two from each state, who serve for six-year terms (one-third of the Senate is up for election every two years). Candidates for the Senate must be at least 30 years old, have been a U.S. citizen for at least nine years, and be a resident of the state from which they are elected.

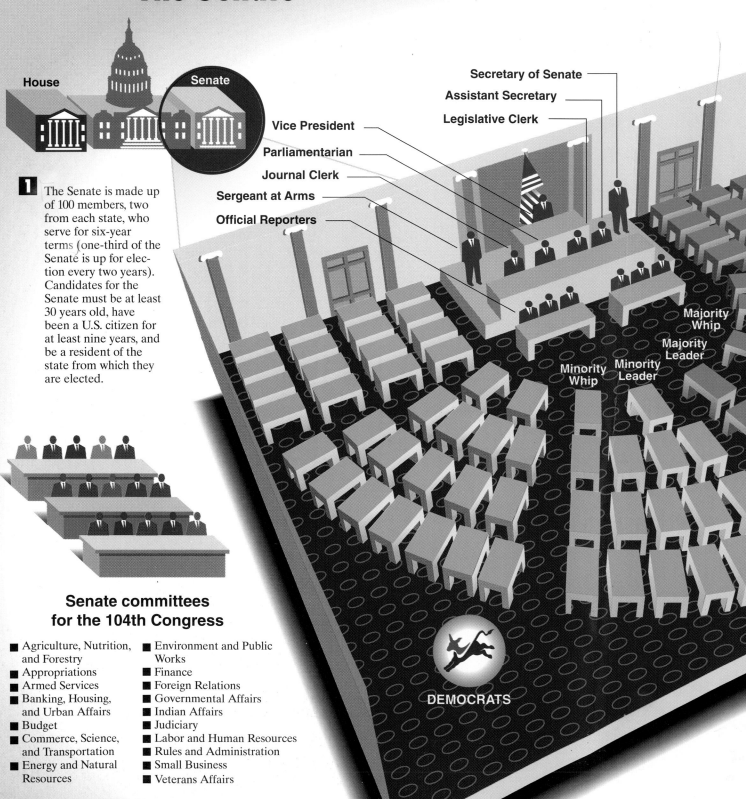

Secretary of Senate

Assistant Secretary

Legislative Clerk

Vice President

Parliamentarian

Journal Clerk

Sergeant at Arms

Official Reporters

Majority Whip

Majority Leader

Minority Whip

Minority Leader

DEMOCRATS

Senate committees for the 104th Congress

- Agriculture, Nutrition, and Forestry
- Appropriations
- Armed Services
- Banking, Housing, and Urban Affairs
- Budget
- Commerce, Science, and Transportation
- Energy and Natural Resources
- Environment and Public Works
- Finance
- Foreign Relations
- Governmental Affairs
- Indian Affairs
- Judiciary
- Labor and Human Resources
- Rules and Administration
- Small Business
- Veterans Affairs

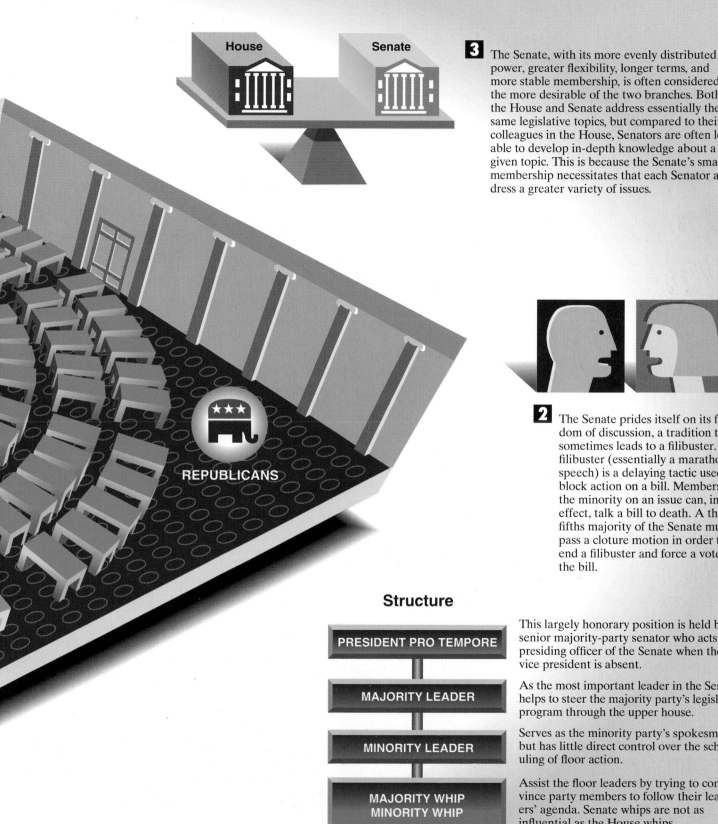

3 The Senate, with its more evenly distributed power, greater flexibility, longer terms, and more stable membership, is often considered the more desirable of the two branches. Both the House and Senate address essentially the same legislative topics, but compared to their colleagues in the House, Senators are often less able to develop in-depth knowledge about a given topic. This is because the Senate's smaller membership necessitates that each Senator address a greater variety of issues.

2 The Senate prides itself on its freedom of discussion, a tradition that sometimes leads to a filibuster. A filibuster (essentially a marathon speech) is a delaying tactic used to block action on a bill. Members in the minority on an issue can, in effect, talk a bill to death. A three-fifths majority of the Senate must pass a cloture motion in order to end a filibuster and force a vote on the bill.

Structure

PRESIDENT PRO TEMPORE

This largely honorary position is held by a senior majority-party senator who acts as presiding officer of the Senate when the vice president is absent.

MAJORITY LEADER

As the most important leader in the Senate, helps to steer the majority party's legislative program through the upper house.

MINORITY LEADER

Serves as the minority party's spokesman but has little direct control over the scheduling of floor action.

MAJORITY WHIP
MINORITY WHIP

Assist the floor leaders by trying to convince party members to follow their leaders' agenda. Senate whips are not as influential as the House whips.

The House of Representatives

House

Senate

1 The House is made up of 435 members who serve for terms of two years. The number of representatives for each state varies and is based on population. Candidates for the House must be at least 25 years old, have been a U.S. citizen for at least seven years, and be a resident of the state from which they are elected. Each congressional district has roughly half a million constituents. States are typically redistricted after each census to reflect population increases or decreases.

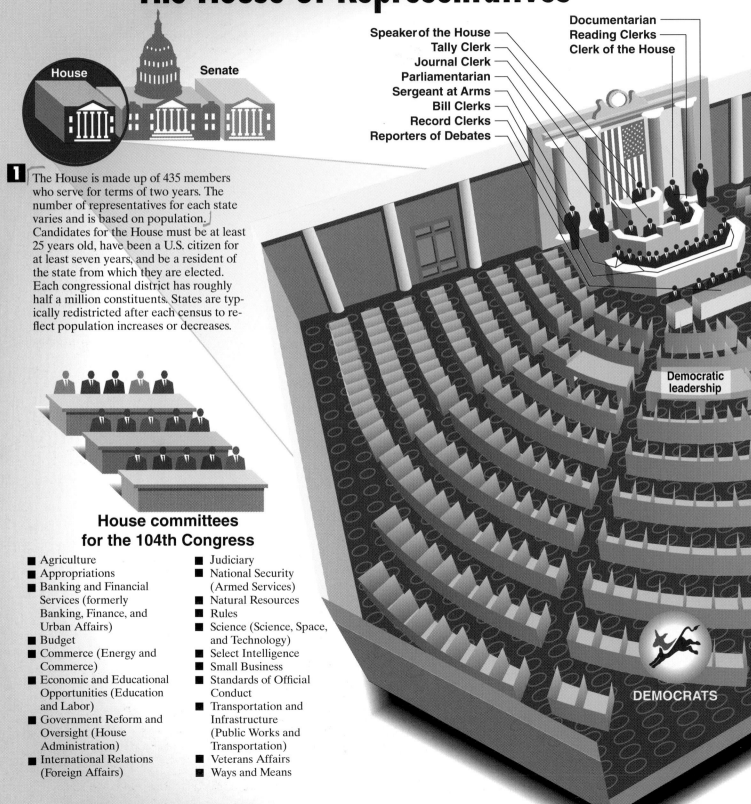

Speaker of the House
Tally Clerk
Journal Clerk
Parliamentarian
Sergeant at Arms
Bill Clerks
Record Clerks
Reporters of Debates

Documentarian
Reading Clerks
Clerk of the House

Democratic leadership

DEMOCRATS

House committees for the 104th Congress

- Agriculture
- Appropriations
- Banking and Financial Services (formerly Banking, Finance, and Urban Affairs)
- Budget
- Commerce (Energy and Commerce)
- Economic and Educational Opportunities (Education and Labor)
- Government Reform and Oversight (House Administration)
- International Relations (Foreign Affairs)

- Judiciary
- National Security (Armed Services)
- Natural Resources
- Rules
- Science (Science, Space, and Technology)
- Select Intelligence
- Small Business
- Standards of Official Conduct
- Transportation and Infrastructure (Public Works and Transportation)
- Veterans Affairs
- Ways and Means

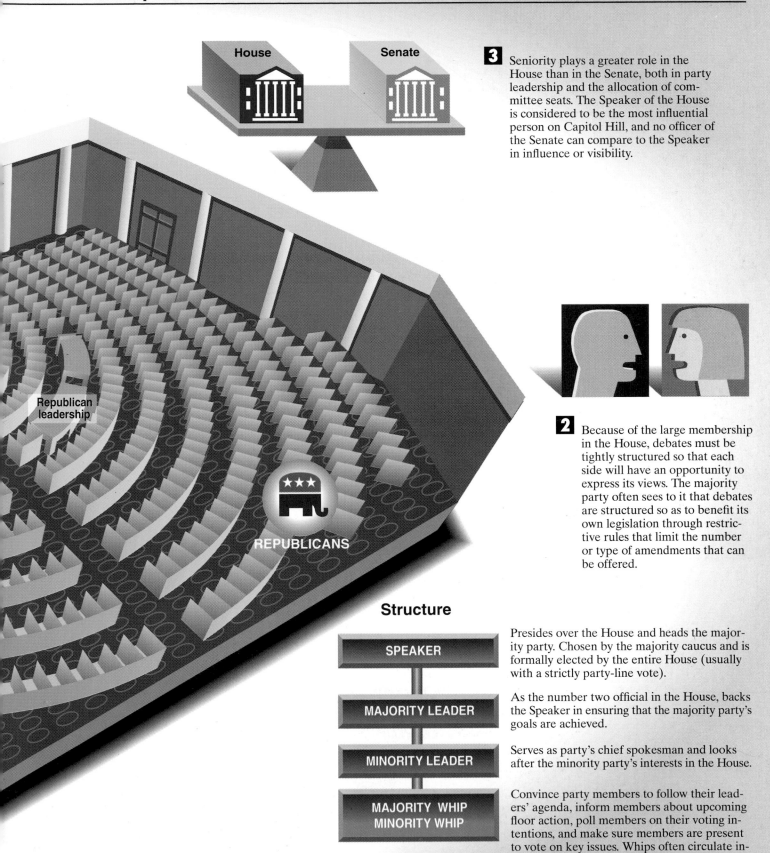

House

Senate

3 Seniority plays a greater role in the House than in the Senate, both in party leadership and the allocation of committee seats. The Speaker of the House is considered to be the most influential person on Capitol Hill, and no officer of the Senate can compare to the Speaker in influence or visibility.

Republican leadership

★★★
REPUBLICANS

2 Because of the large membership in the House, debates must be tightly structured so that each side will have an opportunity to express its views. The majority party often sees to it that debates are structured so as to benefit its own legislation through restrictive rules that limit the number or type of amendments that can be offered.

Structure

Presides over the House and heads the majority party. Chosen by the majority caucus and is formally elected by the entire House (usually with a strictly party-line vote).

SPEAKER

As the number two official in the House, backs the Speaker in ensuring that the majority party's goals are achieved.

MAJORITY LEADER

Serves as party's chief spokesman and looks after the minority party's interests in the House.

MINORITY LEADER

Convince party members to follow their leaders' agenda, inform members about upcoming floor action, poll members on their voting intentions, and make sure members are present to vote on key issues. Whips often circulate informational advisories on legislative and political issues that help to foster party unity.

MAJORITY WHIP
MINORITY WHIP

Congressional Staff and Support Agencies

THE CONGRESSIONAL BUREAUCRACY enhances the ability of legislators to develop policy and make laws. Members are assisted in service to their constituents and the legislative process by both personal and committee staff. In addition to their staff, members are served by several major, nonpartisan agencies: the Library of Congress, the Congressional Budget Office, the General Accounting Office, the Office of Technology Assessment, and the Government Printing Office.

A member's *personal staff* are generally divided between the Washington office and one or more offices in the district. Each office is different, but typically, the Washington staff concentrate their efforts on legislative issues while the district staff focus more on constituent services.

The size of congressional staffs and their responsibilities have expanded greatly over the years. Originally, members of Congress had no staffs at all! Because it is virtually impossible for members to be thoroughly versed on every proposal that comes before them in Congress, staff are needed to monitor legislation, draft proposals, write speeches, answer letters, and negotiate compromises— tasks that were once performed by the members themselves.

Working on a member's personal staff can be truly exciting. Perhaps most significant is the opportunity to actually help shape national policy. Within offices, state delegations, and political parties, a strong camaraderie often develops among staff. The atmosphere can be likened to that of a college campus, complete with the "crunch" periods when bills are coming fast and furious to the floor, and breaks during times of summer or holiday recess. On the downside, the hours are invariably long, salaries are completely at the member's discretion, offices are crowded, and job security depends on the member winning the next election.

A creative staff can do a great deal to keep the legislator in the public eye, thus enhancing the chances for reelection. Positions within a congressional office vary somewhat from office to office, but they typically include the following:

The administrative assistant functions as the member's right arm by overseeing all office operations, determining who will get access to the member, and maintaining communications with important constituents, donors, and key groups and businesses within the district. Often the person who holds this post was the member's campaign manager in a previous election.

The press secretary writes press releases about the member's legislative activities, prepares the newsletters that are sent to constituents, screens requests for interviews, and handles questions from the media.

Legislative assistants cover issues within broad subject areas (such as the environment, defense, or senior citizens), track legislation, and brief the member on the status of legislation, positions taken by relevant interest groups, and the impact proposals might have on the home district. Legislative assistants work with legislative counsel to draft bills. They are often responsible for getting cosponsors for their boss's legislation, meeting with lobbyists and constituents, and answering constituent letters.

Legislative correspondents are typically found in Senate offices and respond to the mountains of mail received by members each day.

Caseworkers are the member's bread and butter. They provide crucial constituent services—helping solve problems constituents have with the federal government. This might include obtaining veterans' or Social Security benefits, facilitating the approval process for a small business loan or award of a federal contract, obtaining an emergency leave from the military, or dealing with the Immigration and Naturalization Service.

Members generally have one scheduler for the Washington office and another for district appointments.

Committee staff do a great deal of Congress's legislative work and can be quite influential in shaping policy. The professional committee staff concentrate on narrow issues within the jurisdiction of the committee on which they serve and are usually well-educated experts in their field. Not surprisingly, these positions are quite a bit more prestigious than personal staff jobs. Clerical staff are responsible for maintaining the committee calendar, filing, processing committee publications, and preparing for hearings.

Major responsibilities of committee staff include organizing hearings, selecting witnesses, structuring investigations, briefing committee members, researching issues that come before the committee, traveling to regions affected by proposals under review, preparing committee reports (often the only reference material available on matters under consideration), comparing proposed bills to existing laws, forming coalitions to support legislation, and preparing legislation for floor action.

Both the Senate and the House of Representatives have an *Office of Legislative Counsel*. They are a critical resource for drafting legislation. Legislative counsel puts the proposals of members and their staffs into legislative language, determines whether or not a proposed bill is in conflict with the Code of Federal Regulations and is consistent with extant legislation and court precedents. Legislative counsel may suggest alternatives to the legislator's original idea.

The *growth and power* of congressional staff is an issue that is of constant concern, especially in these budget-conscious times. Staff growth comes in part from the need for increasing amounts of information on an ever-growing number of issues. The more staff a member of Congress has, the more legislative areas in which he or she can get involved. This in turn creates the need for even more staff to address the increased workload.

While the growth of congressional staff is an issue that is receiving increasing attention, it is not out of line with staff growth in the executive branch. Keeping in mind the system of checks and balances, it is logical to expect that a gross imbalance of staff between the two branches would likely result in a shifting balance of power.

It is true that staff cannot vote, but they do make their mark on every other aspect of bill passage. Committee staff are sometimes criticized for playing too large a role in the shaping of public policy. As we have seen, they draft legislation, plot floor strategy, and negotiate compromises. However, having a capable legislative staff to work out the minutia permits members to concentrate on the big decisions and resolve the major policy disputes.

The *Library of Congress* has two responsibilities: Its first priority is to serve Congress, and secondarily it serves as the nation's library.

Congressional Research Service (CRS), within the Library of Congress, serves Congress by responding to requests from members and their staffs. The services provided by CRS are invaluable and greatly enhance the productivity of congressional staff. On a moment's notice, CRS specialists can provide urgently needed statistics or answer questions in any area of public policy. As a politically neutral organization, CRS does not recommend policy. However, they will research options and determine arguments for or against a proposal. In addition to conducting research, they analyze Supreme Court cases, provide critiques of legislation, or provide articles on any conceivable issue. The only request they will not honor is that of researching political opponents. CRS monitors the status of every major bill before Congress. Summaries of each bill introduced are available in Senate and House offices via computer networks.

To help members better respond to inquiries from their constituents, CRS publishes summaries of many legislative subjects. These reports, issue briefs, and information packs can be ordered by staff and then sent on to a constituent who has requested information on a specific topic.

Anyone may use the Library of Congress without charge, but materials cannot be removed from the library. One of the major services provided to the public by the library is that of cataloging books published in the United States. The catalog number assigned to each book reflects its subject matter. In addition, the Copyright Office records the ownership of literary and other intellectual property; and the library provides services to the blind by distributing books in Braille and on tape.

The *Congressional Budget Office* (CBO) analyzes the budgetary impact of various spending proposals and advises Congress on how much their proposed policies are likely to cost and on how effective the different spending programs are likely to be.

The *General Accounting Office* (GAO) is the oldest and largest congressional support agency. It was established to provide Congress with an independent analysis of executive branch programs (analysis for the executive branch is provided by the Office of Management and Budget) and how the money appropriated by Congress is spent. GAO's role has grown, however. Now, at the request of Congress, GAO will audit or investigate federal agencies and programs and make legislative recommendations for eliminating waste and improving program implementation. Congress may use GAO analyses to justify committee recommendations or refute statistics provided by the administration.

The relatively obscure *Office of Technology Assessment* (OTA) assists Congress in evaluating proposals for scientific and technical legislation. Many of the policies and programs evaluated are narrowly focused, long-term, or extremely technical in nature. For example, OTA might research the international markets for U.S.-made electronics or evaluate proposals to build a coal slurry pipeline.

The *Government Printing Office* (GPO) publishes the mountains of documents generated by Congress and the rest of the federal government. Among the publications that roll off the presses of GPO are the *Congressional Record* (the only official record of congressional proceedings), the *Congressional Directory* (a who's who of Congress containing biographies, phone numbers, staff lists, and other useful information), bills, public laws, members' stationery, and franked envelopes. GPO is one of the largest printing operations in the world, and many of the books, reports, and pamphlets it prints are available for public purchase.

Congressional Staff and Support Agencies

A member's personal staff enhances his or her position in the district by providing constituent services, developing legislative proposals to address local or national issues, and maintaining a favorable public image.

Committee staff experts are influential in shaping public policy. They conduct hearings, resolve differences between Senate and House versions of the same legislation, form coalitions in support of legislative proposals, and brief members in preparation for floor action.

The Congressional Budget Office advises Congress on the likely effect of different spending proposals and provides members with cost estimates for new policies.

The Government Accounting Office has been described as a "watchdog" and is responsible for overseeing executive branch expenditures and evaluating executive branch programs for Congress.

The Library of Congress, and especially its Congressional Research Service, furnishes members with unbiased information used in the legislative process or to respond to constituent inquiries and answers questions on every conceivable issue for both members and their staffs.

The Office of Technology Assessment assists Congress in evaluating proposals for scientific and technical legislation.

The Government Printing Office publishes documents for Congress and the federal government. Many of these publications are available for purchase by the public.

How Congressional Staff Shape Legislation

1 Legislative assistants are constantly on the lookout for local or national issues that might be addressed through legislation. They then suggest proposals to their bosses, poll groups and perhaps individuals to determine if there is (or isn't) support for the proposal, research any aspects that may have been overlooked, and search for those who might be adversely affected and determine how seriously. Throughout, staff make extensive use of the considerable resources available to members of Congress, for example, Congressional Research Service, General Accounting Office, and Congressional Budget Office.

2 Members' staff consult with legislative counsel in order to determine where the new proposal fits in with current law. Legislative counsel drafts the legislation according to the wishes of the members and their staff representatives, and in light of existing laws.

3 Committee staff schedule hearings, complete with testimony from expert witnesses and those who may be adversely affected. The legislation is fine-tuned in response to information gleaned during the hearing process.

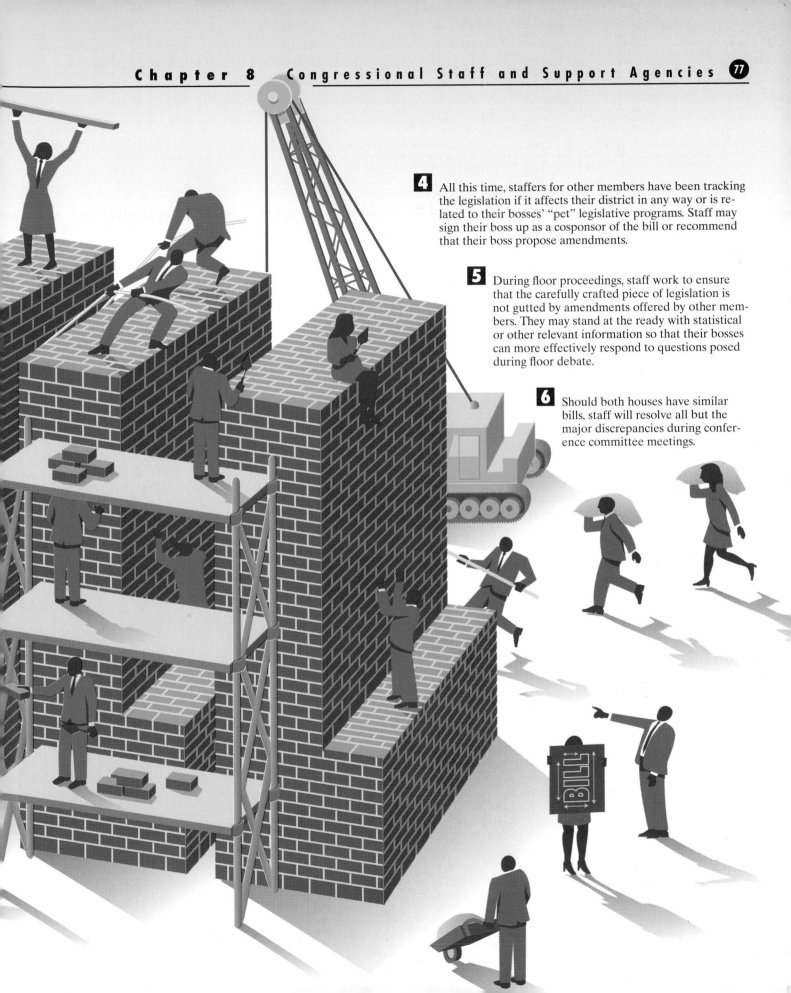

4 All this time, staffers for other members have been tracking the legislation if it affects their district in any way or is related to their bosses' "pet" legislative programs. Staff may sign their boss up as a cosponsor of the bill or recommend that their boss propose amendments.

5 During floor proceedings, staff work to ensure that the carefully crafted piece of legislation is not gutted by amendments offered by other members. They may stand at the ready with statistical or other relevant information so that their bosses can more effectively respond to questions posed during floor debate.

6 Should both houses have similar bills, staff will resolve all but the major discrepancies during conference committee meetings.

The Legislative Process

THE LEGISLATIVE PROCESS from the introduction of a bill to the enactment of a law can take months, or even years. It takes time to gain consensus, accommodate different interests, strike bargains, and form coalitions. While outside observers may be impatient with the pace of Congress, this slowness promotes fairness, giving interested constituencies a better opportunity to be heard.

The mechanism for developing national budget policy changed dramatically with the Congressional Budget and Impoundment Control Act of 1974. Prior to this, presidents could *impound* (refuse to spend) money that Congress had appropriated and thus assume greater control of agency activities. Today, concern over budget cuts in areas the public has come to rely heavily upon generates a great deal of interest in the budget process. Because budgetary concerns have a significant impact on the types of bills that are likely to pass, the highlights of the budget process will be discussed later in this chapter.

Only a small percentage of the bills introduced in Congress are ever enacted into law. According to the Congressional Research Service, 10,238 bills and joint resolutions were introduced during the 102nd Congress. Of these, only 590 became law.

Sources of legislative proposals include the executive branch, interest groups, political parties, members themselves, constituents, and business groups. Sometimes they originate as campaign promises. Others are based on a need to change, repeal, or completely revise existing laws. Many bills are introduced more with the idea of publicizing an issue and generating interest than with the intent of actually enacting a new law.

Major proposals on the legislative agenda generally come from the president or from executive branch agencies. The president cannot introduce legislation himself, but he often gets credit for proposals that have been kicking around Congress for years. An "executive communication" in the form of a letter from a cabinet member, agency head, or even the president, is used to transmit a draft legislative proposal to the Speaker of the House and president of the Senate. This communication is then referred as a bill to the appropriate committee(s). Not every executive branch directive makes it to the floor. Many result in a study by a commission or committee designated by the president or a cabinet officer.

There are four types of legislative proposals. A *bill* is the form used most often for legislation. A *joint resolution* (so-called, although it does not necessarily have to be introduced jointly as the name implies) may originate in either house and is essentially the same as a bill, but with a more limited focus. Joint resolutions are typically used for proposed constitutional amendments, special appropriations, and making minor or technical changes in newly enacted legislation or existing law. A *concurrent resolution* is not usually legislative, but instead relates to the operations of both houses and is not presented to the president. A *simple resolution* concerns matters in just one house and is considered in that house only.

In order to get support for a proposal, staff research potential allies, poll those active in the field, and develop a network of individuals and groups who are in favor of the idea. To get as many members as possible to cosponsor the bill, legislative assistants may circulate "Dear Colleague" letters prior to its introduction and throughout the legislative process. In addition, staff may compile information—in such forms as fact sheets, news clippings, or statements from organizations both in favor of and opposed to the bill—for members (and other groups) who are interested in the measure but would like additional information before making a commitment.

Each bill must be introduced by a member of the House or Senate. House members introduce a bill by putting it in the "hopper" near the clerk's desk. Senators generally introduce a bill by presenting it to a clerk at the presiding officer's desk. Often a member will make a statement on the floor announcing the introduction of his or her bill and outlining its merits.

The member who has introduced a bill may continue to promote the legislation during floor speeches and by submitting statements to be published in the Congressional Record. The member's press secretary may write op-ed pieces for the local (and perhaps national) newspapers and field questions from interested media.

Once a bill is introduced, it is referred to one or more committees or subcommittees. Committees are the most important part of the legislative process. This is where the most intensive negotiations take place and where the public is given an opportunity to voice opinions.

Not every bill referred to committee is acted upon. For those measures that are considered, hearings are held to determine what the arguments are (and how intense they are), for and against, to decide whether the legislation is even necessary, and to negotiate amendments prior to floor consideration. Should extensive revisions be necessary, the committee might develop an entirely new piece of legislation (known as a clean bill), which must then be reintroduced and referred back to the committee.

After all viewpoints have been studied in detail, the bill is *marked-up*, or edited. During committee (or subcommittee) mark-up, the bill is reviewed line by line, adding or deleting provisions as necessary. The expertise of committee staff is invaluable at this stage. The marked-up bill is considered one last time by the full committee, who may (1) recommend that it be considered by the full House or Senate with or without amendments (this is known as "reporting" the bill, or favorably reporting the bill); (2) rule against reporting the bill out; or (3) suggest tabling (indefinitely postponing action) the legislation.

Amendments that were not adopted during the committee process may be offered again on the floor, and provisions adopted in committee may be deleted.

Decisions made in committee are critical to the success or failure of a bill. Once a bill has been reported out of committee, it has an excellent chance for passage, even though it might be changed again by amendments during floor debate.

A *committee report* is written for bills that have been reported favorably. This document indicates the changes proposed in existing law and what each section of the bill is intended to accomplish. It is an important part of a bill's legislative history and is considered by the executive and judicial branches as a statement of the Congress's intent regarding how the law is to be implemented.

Before a bill can be brought to the floor of the House, the Committee on Rules must grant a rule that (1) determines when the bill will be considered by the full house, (2) provides guidelines for debate, and (3) in some cases governs how many and what kinds of amendments may be offered. A "closed rule" is one that does not allow amendments to be offered. The committee may occasionally refuse to grant a rule, which in effect kills the legislation.

When a bill is considered on the floor of the House, debate is tightly controlled by the rule. In the Senate, debate is unlimited—occasionally, senators may even try to defeat a bill by talking it to death in what is known as a *filibuster* (see Chapter 7). It is during floor consideration that amendments are offered, incorporated, or defeated, and a vote is taken on final passage of the legislation as amended.

Several hundred votes are recorded during each session of Congress. The way in which members cast their votes reflects their backgrounds, constituencies, values, and party affiliation—as well as compromises they have made. Often there is more to why members vote the way they do than meets the eye. This is most evident when the yeas and nays are taken on an *omnibus bill* (many unrelated proposals bundled into a single piece of legislation, also referred to as a "Christmas Tree" bill for the many "ornaments" that are attached) rather than on a piece of legislation that addresses a single issue.

On final passage (especially of complex, omnibus bills) it is not at all unusual for a member to be caught in a double bind. For example, the member must either vote *for* legislation that contains objectionable provisions or vote *against* legislation that would, in part, benefit his or her constituents. For this reason, claims that "Congressman Smith voted against lunches for hungry school children" should be taken with the proverbial grain of salt. Congressman Smith may strongly favor the school lunch program but have been unwilling to support "Christmas tree" legislation added to the school lunch bill that provided generous tax breaks to the committee chairman's best buddy back home.

If, in spite of floor amendments, a bill is defeated in one chamber, but passed in another, committees in both houses may try to rewrite the legislation in order to make it less objectionable. Politics does play a role and a bill that easily passes in one house may never get the necessary votes in the other until the balance of those for and against shifts (this may take more than one election cycle). Time constraints are always a consideration. If suitable language for the bill cannot be agreed upon before Congress adjourns, the process must begin again when the next Congress convenes. Because so much legislative negotiating is done in committees, the majority of bills that are sent to the floor eventually win passage. However, it is not unusual for a proposal to be debated on the floor of one or both chambers in several successive congresses.

Should a House-Senate conference be expected (to resolve differences between the bills approved in each chamber), certain points that one chamber might otherwise vote out may be left in to be used later as bargaining chips during conference negotiations. Those in strong support of points they believe might be sacrificed in conference may call for roll-call votes on these amendments. A strong margin in favor might persuade conferees to retain these points.

On major bills, a conference is virtually assured because each chamber will have passed its own version of the legislation. Before the bill can be sent to the president, all of the differences between the two versions must be resolved. This can be accomplished in several ways. One chamber may adopt the other's version. One bill or the other may be used as a basis for amendments. Or, the conferees may negotiate compromises throughout until the result is a bill with which both sides are comfortable. Most often the conference report is easily adopted by both houses.

The president has several options when presented with a bill that has passed both houses. He can sign it into law, he can allow the bill to become law without his signature (this occurs if the president fails to act on the bill within 10 legislative days), or he can veto it. A presidential veto may be overridden by a two-thirds majority in each house, thus making the bill law without presidential approval. If the president fails to sign a bill passed less than 10 days before congress adjourns, the bill is "pocket vetoed." If the bill is introduced in the next Congress, the legislative process begins again.

How *Does* a Bill Become Law?

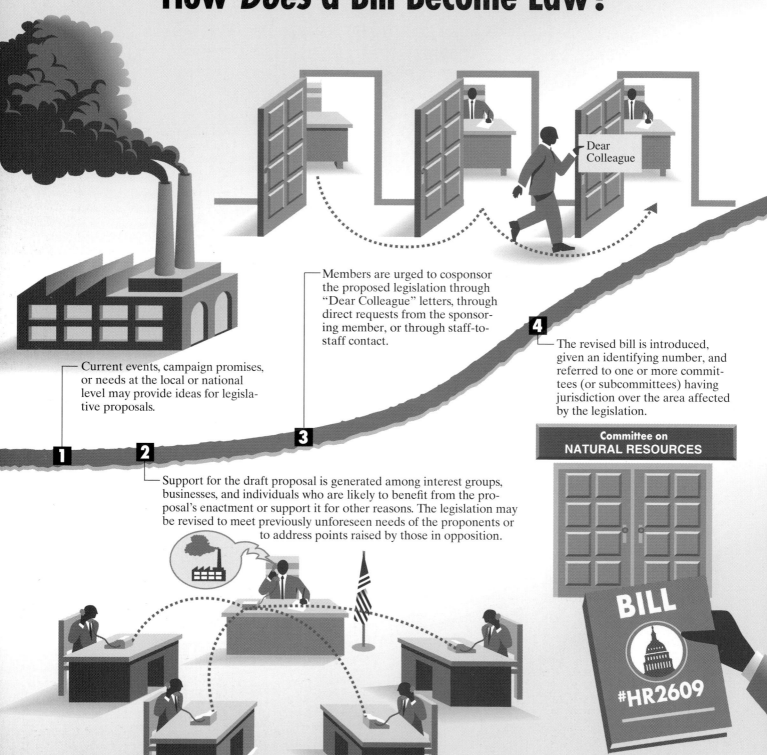

1 Current events, campaign promises, or needs at the local or national level may provide ideas for legislative proposals.

2 Support for the draft proposal is generated among interest groups, businesses, and individuals who are likely to benefit from the proposal's enactment or support it for other reasons. The legislation may be revised to meet previously unforeseen needs of the proponents or to address points raised by those in opposition.

3 Members are urged to cosponsor the proposed legislation through "Dear Colleague" letters, through direct requests from the sponsoring member, or through staff-to-staff contact.

4 The revised bill is introduced, given an identifying number, and referred to one or more committees (or subcommittees) having jurisdiction over the area affected by the legislation.

Dear Colleague

Committee on **NATURAL RESOURCES**

BILL #HR2609

In committee, hearings are held on the legislation, amendments are adopted or rejected, the bill is "marked-up" (edited) in preparation for floor consideration, and a committee report is written describing the intent of the legislation.

5

6

The Committee on Rules in the House, or the majority and minority leaders in the Senate, determine the conditions under which the bill will be debated.

7

During floor debate, amendments may be offered, accepted, or rejected, and a final vote is taken on the legislation as amended. If passed, the bill is referred to the other chamber for committee, and then floor consideration.

8

If the other chamber is considering similar legislation (or has already passed it) both versions, once passed, will be sent to a conference committee in order to resolve any differences.

9

Both houses must approve the exact same version of a bill before it can be sent to the president for his approval or veto.

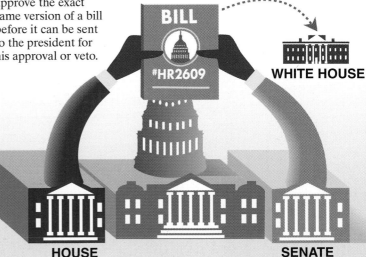

WHITE HOUSE

HOUSE

SENATE

The Budget Process in Brief

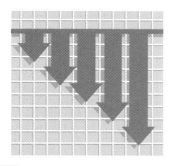

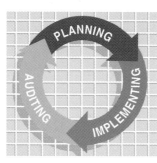

1 Budget issues have increasingly dominated political discussions and can be expected to remain in the spotlight because of the public's continued frustration with high deficits and the apparent difficulty of either increasing revenue or cutting spending. Growing concern for deficit spending and the cost of servicing our national debt have prompted several legislative measures, most notably the Gramm-Rudman-Hollings Balanced Budget Act of 1985.

2 The budget process is virtually continuous, with both the executive and legislative branches planning the next budget, implementing the current budget, and auditing the previous fiscal year.

3 The president's budget is prepared by the Office of Management and Budget in consultation with other federal government departments and agencies. Policy goals are weighed, past spending is reviewed along with requests for new funding, and the state of the economy is taken into consideration.

4 The president's budget includes spending and revenue projections for the next five years. While factors such as employment, inflation, or international crisis can influence future budgets, these projections are nonetheless used as guidelines by executive agencies and Congress for future planning and as an indication of the long-term effects of current spending.

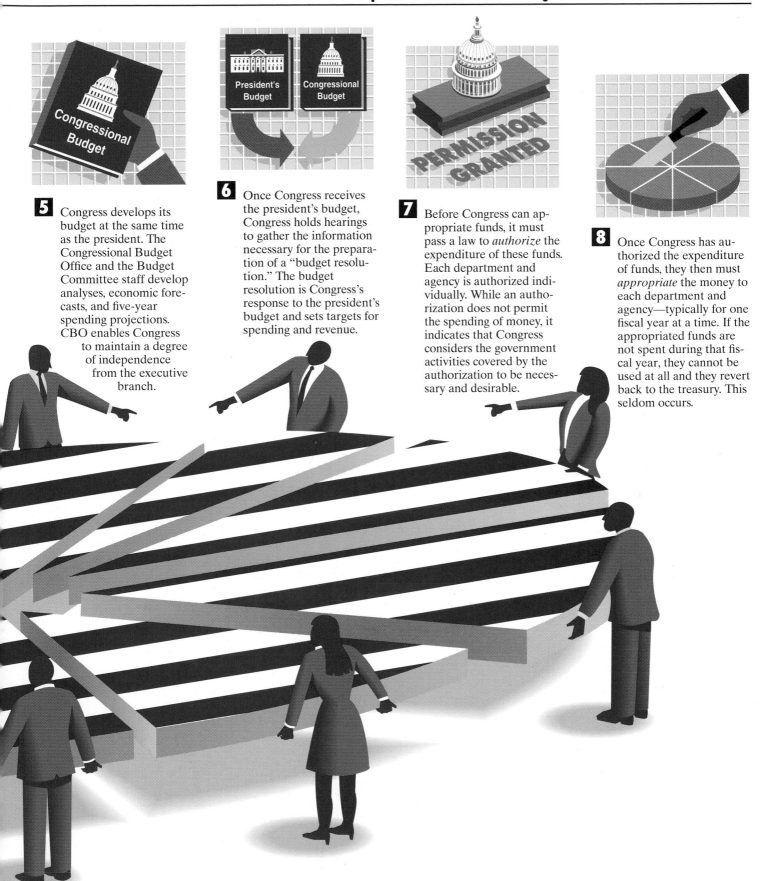

5 Congress develops its budget at the same time as the president. The Congressional Budget Office and the Budget Committee staff develop analyses, economic forecasts, and five-year spending projections. CBO enables Congress to maintain a degree of independence from the executive branch.

6 Once Congress receives the president's budget, Congress holds hearings to gather the information necessary for the preparation of a "budget resolution." The budget resolution is Congress's response to the president's budget and sets targets for spending and revenue.

7 Before Congress can appropriate funds, it must pass a law to *authorize* the expenditure of these funds. Each department and agency is authorized individually. While an authorization does not permit the spending of money, it indicates that Congress considers the government activities covered by the authorization to be necessary and desirable.

8 Once Congress has authorized the expenditure of funds, they then must *appropriate* the money to each department and agency—typically for one fiscal year at a time. If the appropriated funds are not spent during that fiscal year, they cannot be used at all and they revert back to the treasury. This seldom occurs.

Lobbyists and Interest Groups

N THE WORDS of the late Speaker of the House, Thomas P. (Tip) O'Neill, "All politics is local." Members of Congress are always aware that without the voters at home, they would not be in office. It is the tendency of these voters to organize into *interest groups* in order to more powerfully convey their ideas and concerns to representatives in Washington.

An interest group is any organization that seeks to influence public policy. Depending on what the membership wants, a group's goals can be narrowly defined or quite broad. The number and variety of special interest groups is considerable. There are groups reflecting concerns of business and labor, agriculture, professionals, and consumers, groups reflecting social and political concerns, and groups that champion those who cannot help themselves, as well as countless others.

The American Association of Retired Persons (AARP) is unusual in that it is a remarkably large interest group whose membership cuts across many demographic lines.

Organized groups use lobbyists to help them convey their message to legislators. Professional lobbyists tend to be well-educated experts in their field. Larger interest groups often have offices in Washington and several full-time lobbyists on staff. Should a group be too small to justify its own Washington office, or perhaps have only a one-time need for a lobbyist, it might hire a professional lobbyist to represent it.

Every issue imaginable attracts the attention of competing interest groups, and they (and the lobbyists who represent them) have become a powerful force in our political process. Most major legislative proposals are not only supported by groups who want change, they are opposed by equally powerful groups who may want altogether different changes, or no change at all.

A successful lobbyist will not only be well-versed in a given area of expertise, he or she will know the ins and outs of the legislative process. Contrary to popular opinion, lobbyists seldom present only the positive aspects of their legislative proposals. By providing complete and accurate information, being honest about what a proposal will and will not do, and alerting members to any negative aspects, lobbyists build and maintain working relationships with members and staff based on trust that will often continue for many years.

Lobbyists rely on both direct and indirect lobbying techniques. Direct lobbying consists of face-to-face meetings with members and their staffs. Indirect lobbying is more commonly termed "grass roots lobbying" and consists of lobbyists or groups generating interest among members of the public, who will then contact legislators and urge them to act. Both of these techniques are used successfully by interest groups.

Grass roots support for an issue is nearly always spurred by the efforts of interest groups. When public opinion is strongly behind a legislative proposal, it usually passes; therefore, interest groups expend a great deal of their resources motivating voters around the country to stand behind their causes.

Interest groups can exert political pressure because they have a vast store of detailed information and are a prime source of expertise. The size and wealth of an interest group are not the only indicators of power. The most influential groups are also able to consistently stimulate letter-writing campaigns (which are easily recognized as such by members and staff), generate headlines, and even stage demonstrations when necessary.

Not every interest group is as it seems. Often, those directly involved in an issue and on Capitol Hill know whose money is behind what group, but the public can be easily swept along by groups that use misleading names. A recent example of how interest groups can disguise their real objectives occurred in the early 1990s. California enacted a ban on smoking in public buildings, and the public was hit with a barrage of advertising informing them that restaurants would lose significant amounts of business if this ban were enforced. What was not spoken was that the oft-quoted studies were hardly scientific, and that the tobacco industry was paying for ads that appeared to come from the restaurant industry!

A century ago, lobbyists were thought of as unscrupulous characters who lurked outside hearing rooms in hopes of catching members who would accept bribes. After World War II, the image of vote-buying lobbyists was gradually replaced as lobbyists began to use more sophisticated techniques such as grass roots lobbying and generation of political support at election time. Today, lobbyists have a somewhat more positive image as increasingly they provide the public with information on problems in society and stimulate public debate.

Congress has tried to impose restrictions on lobbying, often in response to scandal, by passing laws that require lobbyists to register with the Clerk of the House and Secretary of the Senate and file quarterly financial reports. It is extraordinarily difficult to impose effective restrictions on lobbyists and lobbying without infringing on the constitutional rights of free speech, assembly, and petition of government. Because of numerous loopholes (for example, not all who lobby are required to register, and financial statements do not always accurately reflect expenditures) the actual effect of restrictions already in effect is debatable. To circumvent some of the restrictions on political contributions, many interest groups have formed Political Action Committees (PACs). Campaign contributions may help to make a member more receptive to an interest group's legislative agenda, but more often they are presented as helping to ensure that members who are supportive of an interest group's ideals will remain in office.

Who Lobbies Congress?

The formation of interest groups can help individuals shape legislative decisions that affect their lives. Not all interests groups are equal in power. A group's size, cohesiveness, and financial base and the compatibility of its goals to those of society as a whole are among the factors that influence how successful the group will be in its efforts to sway government.

There are hundreds of trade associations that seek regulations to enhance conditions for their area of business. The U.S. Chamber of Commerce and the National Association of Manufacturers are the best known business interest groups. But, many a firm like AT&T, General Electric, Proctor & Gamble, Ford, Nabisco, or Exxon is large and influential enough to serve as an interest group in and of itself.

Governments even lobby each other. The National Governors Association, U.S. Conference of Mayors, National League of Cities, and National Association of Counties are among the most notable of these groups. Many states and cities have their own Washington representatives. The president's congressional liaison staff promotes his agenda, and many of the executive departments and agencies have their own congressional relations staffs.

Single-issue groups include the National Rifle Association and Mothers Against Drunk Driving. Their high visibility and narrow focus helps them to play an increasingly important role in politics.

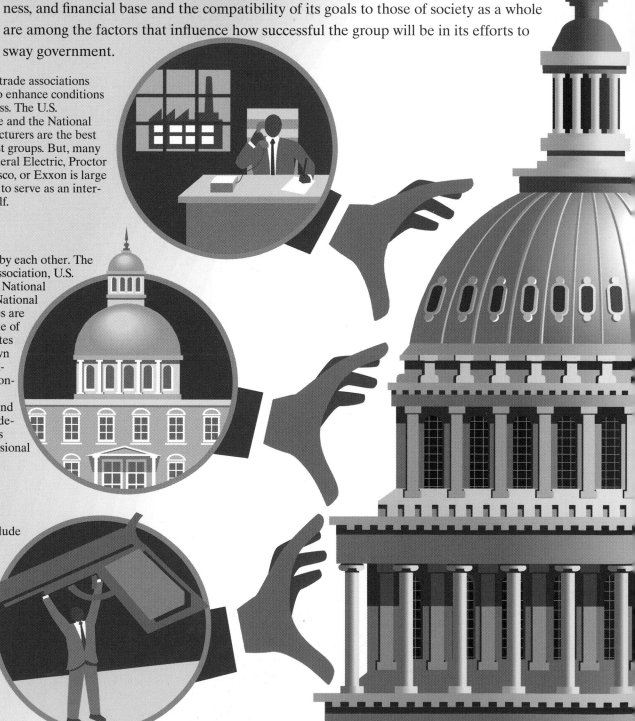

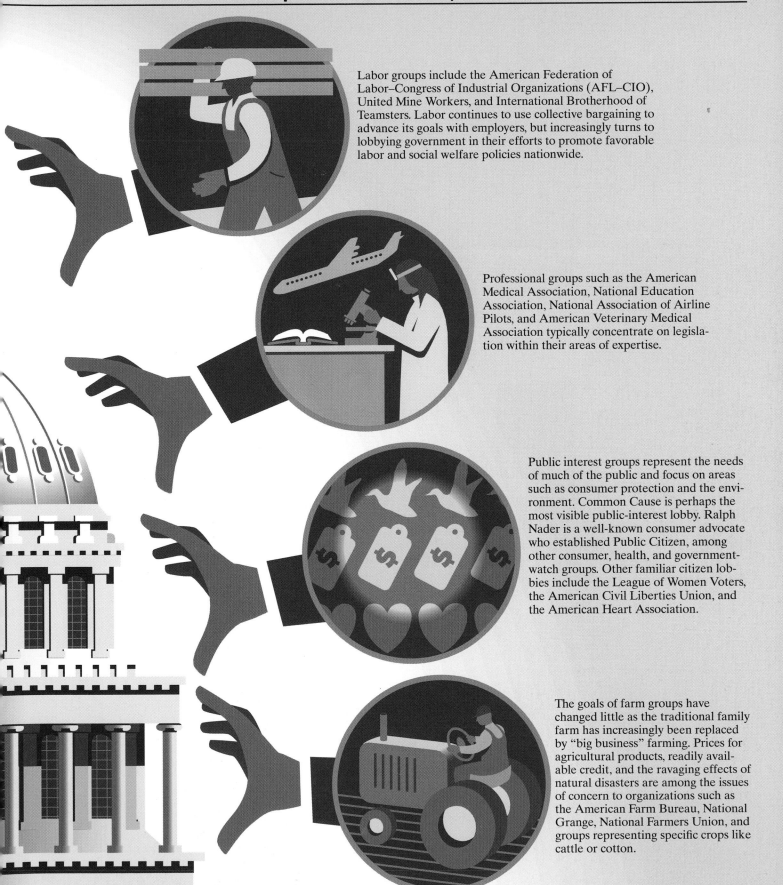

Labor groups include the American Federation of Labor–Congress of Industrial Organizations (AFL–CIO), United Mine Workers, and International Brotherhood of Teamsters. Labor continues to use collective bargaining to advance its goals with employers, but increasingly turns to lobbying government in their efforts to promote favorable labor and social welfare policies nationwide.

Professional groups such as the American Medical Association, National Education Association, National Association of Airline Pilots, and American Veterinary Medical Association typically concentrate on legislation within their areas of expertise.

Public interest groups represent the needs of much of the public and focus on areas such as consumer protection and the environment. Common Cause is perhaps the most visible public-interest lobby. Ralph Nader is a well-known consumer advocate who established Public Citizen, among other consumer, health, and government-watch groups. Other familiar citizen lobbies include the League of Women Voters, the American Civil Liberties Union, and the American Heart Association.

The goals of farm groups have changed little as the traditional family farm has increasingly been replaced by "big business" farming. Prices for agricultural products, readily available credit, and the ravaging effects of natural disasters are among the issues of concern to organizations such as the American Farm Bureau, National Grange, National Farmers Union, and groups representing specific crops like cattle or cotton.

How Do Lobbyists Influence Congress?

The primary goal of lobbyists is to influence the decisions made by government. Lobbyists must negotiate with other interest groups, as well as Congress, in order to achieve their goals. Successful lobbyists build coalitions, are well organized, open to new ideas, and know when to compromise. Lobbyists tend to focus their efforts on legislators who are already friendly to their cause because very few members reverse their position on issues that are important to them or their constituents.

The face-to-face contact lobbyists have with government officials is known as direct lobbying. Direct lobbying may include meeting with members and staff, devising strategies, and testifying at hearings. Lobbyists assist legislators by providing information on benefits and costs, determining how constituents view a proposal, mediating with other groups, forming coalitions, and drafting legislation.

To generate support for their proposal, lobbyists build coalitions with other like-minded interest groups. Coalitions of interest groups often must compromise on major points and generally iron out most of their differences and map a strategy before presenting a proposal to legislators on Capitol Hill.

Indirect, or grass roots, lobbying seeks to influence government's decisions by working through the public. Grass roots lobbying is designed to move the public to act (by writing or calling their representatives), or to build public support for an issue by providing information and enhancing the peoples' understanding of an issue. Grass roots campaigns may be enhanced through the use of media ads, targeted mailings, editorials, and news stories. Some groups may even seek the advice of public relations firms.

Lobbyists must have a good working relationship with congressional staff in order to be successful. They will provide staff with extensive background information, technical data, and a reasonably objective appraisal of the political climate. Staff are often a tougher audience than the members and will thoroughly review and evaluate a proposal before presenting it to their boss. Lobbyists who provide faulty or misleading information are seldom given a second chance.

Most lobbying is done long before a bill reaches the House or Senate floor. Hearings provide lobbyists with an excellent opportunity to present their case to key legislators who might otherwise have been difficult to reach. The media will take notice of a legislative proposal when it advances to the hearing process. Because the public typically considers issues that make the news to be more compelling, legislators are sometimes forced to place a higher priority on those issues.

House and Senate Elections

MEMBERS OF THE House and Senate represent vastly smaller constituencies than do presidents. Because they are closer to the people who put them in office, they are somewhat more accountable to their voters. The number of constituents who know the candidate (name recognition) and think favorably about the candidate's service, or potential for service, is what really counts in a bid for a Senate or House seat.

While congressional salaries ($133,600 for members of the 104th) seem ample to most Americans, many members of Congress could make substantially more in another line of work. The men and women who seek national office aren't in it for the money, however. They really do want to improve things—of course, everyone has a different idea of what needs improving and how to go about it! Washington, D.C. is a city where things happen. The sense of not only being part of the action, but of actually shaping the action, keeps many office holders running for reelection term after term. (Unless, of course, the office holder hails from one of an increasing number of states that limit the number of terms one may serve.)

Every state is granted two seats in the Senate. House seats, on the other hand, are awarded by population, and limited to a total of 435. The decennial census is used to determine the population of each state, and how that population may have changed in the 10 years since the last census. States are given seats in the House based on the number of residents in that state. States that have experienced an upward shift in population often gain one or more seats in the House, while states that have lost a significant number of residents are likely to lose seats. Awarding seats based on a state's population is known as *apportionment*. The governors and state legislatures are generally responsible for drawing lines (*redistricting*) for the new congressional districts. Politics typically plays a role in this, and *gerrymandering* is the term used when district lines are drawn in such a way as to benefit a certain party or politician.

We will discuss races for Senate and House seats together, but there are some critical differences to keep in mind. While the reelection schedule for the Senate is more relaxed than that for the House (once every six years as opposed to every two years), Senate races tend to be more competitive than House races. Not only is a senator's constituency more diverse and therefore harder to please, the office is seen as a stepping stone to national prominence, even the presidency, and this attracts more, and better funded, challengers. Senate challengers often find it easier to raise funds than do House challengers. The average cost of winning a congressional seat in the House is about $545,000, compared to $3.5 million in the Senate. Representatives tend to work more closely with their constituents than do senators, so the benefits of incumbency often have a greater influence on House races.

Incumbency is the single most important factor in House and Senate races because those who decide to run again almost always win—the 1994 election notwithstanding. The key advantages to being an incumbent include visibility that is enhanced through town meetings and personal appearances, the opportunity to provide constituent services, and campaign contributions from political action committees (PACs), who seldom contribute to the campaign coffers of unknown challengers. Incumbents can run on their record of service to the district and their promises to continue the good work. Conversely, challengers will attack the incumbent's record and emphasize the need for new and uncorrupted blood in Washington.

House and Senate candidates use political and media consultants just as presidential candidates do, but since all aspects of their campaigns are on a smaller scale, candidates in House and Senate races are better able to make personal contact and establish a bond with their voters.

Local newspapers often get involved in Senate and House races to a greater degree than just straight reporting on events and may endorse candidates or conduct a "truth watch" in which campaign advertisements are evaluated. However, voters generally get most of their information from television.

A typical campaign office for a Senate or House candidate might be headed by a professional campaign manager, a key person on an incumbent's staff, or a long-time friend or business associate who is familiar with the politics of the district and knows many of the local political players and big donors personally. The campaign manager is generally assisted by a few paid staff members who take care of fundraising, media relations, the computer system, and answering the phones. Key staff may represent an incumbent at an important town meeting or community event when the member must be in Washington or cannot attend simultaneous events in far corners of the district.

The core campaign staff is supported by an army of volunteers who range from students getting extra credit for their government class, to family members, to supporters who are available for a few hours each week, to recent college graduates who see working on a campaign as a step toward a career in the nation's capital. Campaign volunteers may update donor lists on the computer, assist at fundraisers, answer the phones, call groups and individuals to get out the vote, pound in yard signs, sort and file news clippings having to do with every aspect of the campaign, stuff envelopes, and run errands.

In the final days of a campaign, the office is crowded with enthusiastic well-wishers, and everyone offers to help in any way. If things are especially hectic, this might even mean picking up lunch for harried campaign staffers.

On election night, the candidate and supporters gather for what everyone hopes will be a victory celebration. Supporters monitor the televised election coverage to see how their candidate (and others) are doing in the exit polls. The candidate's party may have gained or lost seats in the House or Senate; in a presidential election year, many marginal candidates can be swept into office on the president's coattails; or there could be a significant shift in which party is in power, as happened in the 1994 election.

Should a race be extremely tight, staff at the campaign's headquarters will anxiously tabulate results as, one by one, the precincts close. The final result of an election may not be known until the next day. When the difference between winning and losing is only a few votes, one of the candidates is likely to request a recount. In fact, many states automatically recount the votes when the margin of victory is below a pre-set figure.

Once victory is assured, the losing candidate will often call to concede the election and congratulate the winner. In a particularly bitter race, however, losers have been known to forgo this mannerly act.

After the election, campaign staff, and perhaps a few dedicated volunteers, will take care of collecting yard signs, sending thank-yous, filing final reports on campaign contributions and expenditures with the Federal Election Commission, and packing up the campaign office.

Incumbents will take time off to be with their families and relax before a new session of Congress begins. New members will begin to select staff for their Washington and district offices and attend countless orientation meetings in the weeks leading up to the swearing in.

Highlights of a Congressional Race

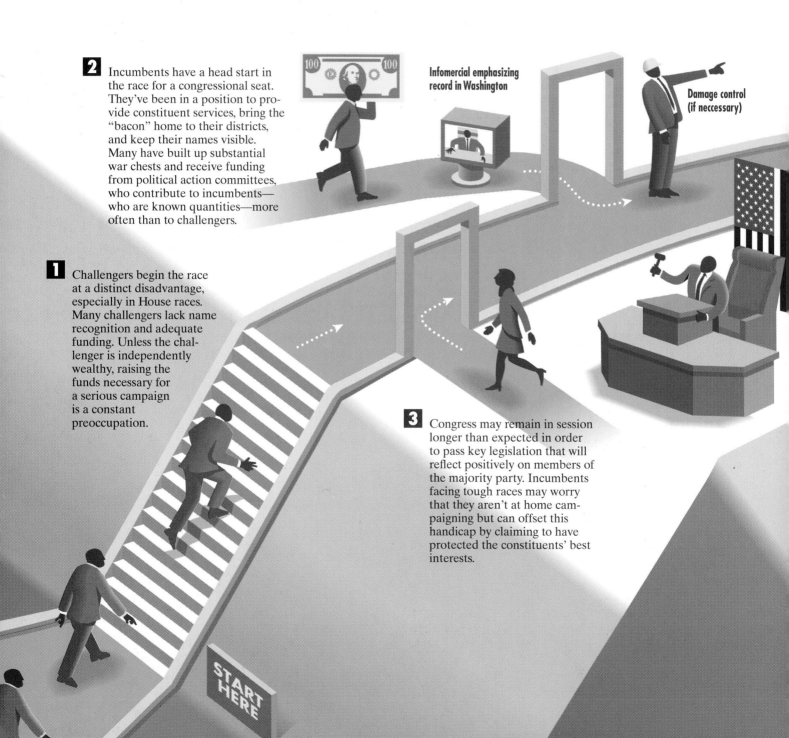

2 Incumbents have a head start in the race for a congressional seat. They've been in a position to provide constituent services, bring the "bacon" home to their districts, and keep their names visible. Many have built up substantial war chests and receive funding from political action committees, who contribute to incumbents— who are known quantities—more often than to challengers.

Infomercial emphasizing record in Washington

Damage control (if neccessary)

1 Challengers begin the race at a distinct disadvantage, especially in House races. Many challengers lack name recognition and adequate funding. Unless the challenger is independently wealthy, raising the funds necessary for a serious campaign is a constant preoccupation.

3 Congress may remain in session longer than expected in order to pass key legislation that will reflect positively on members of the majority party. Incumbents facing tough races may worry that they aren't at home campaigning but can offset this handicap by claiming to have protected the constituents' best interests.

START HERE

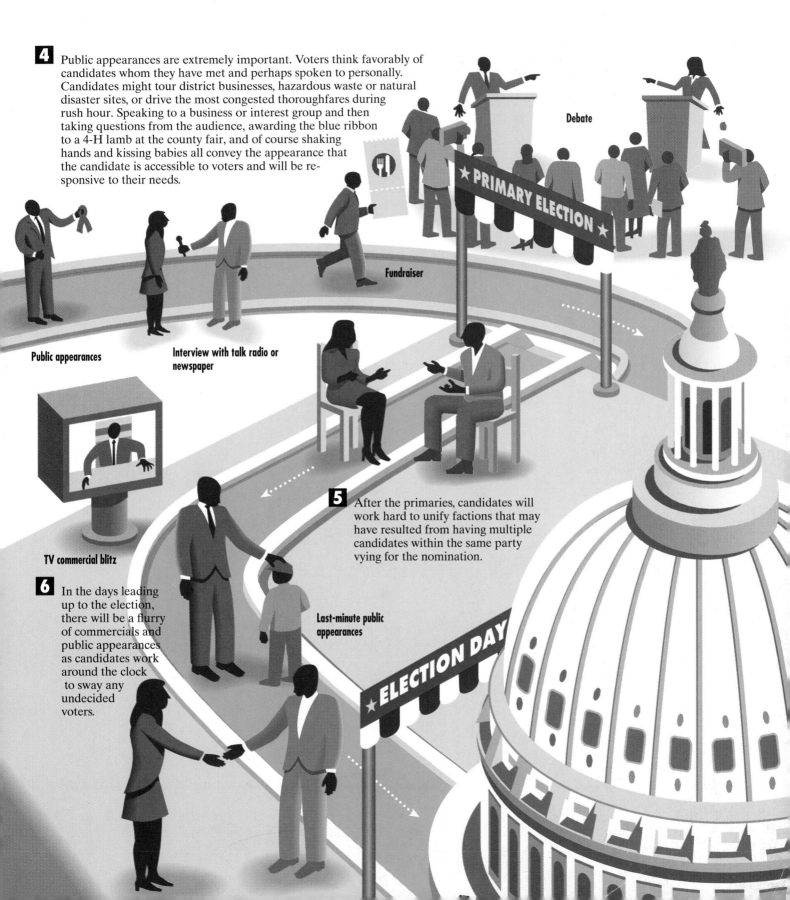

4 Public appearances are extremely important. Voters think favorably of candidates whom they have met and perhaps spoken to personally. Candidates might tour district businesses, hazardous waste or natural disaster sites, or drive the most congested thoroughfares during rush hour. Speaking to a business or interest group and then taking questions from the audience, awarding the blue ribbon to a 4-H lamb at the county fair, and of course shaking hands and kissing babies all convey the appearance that the candidate is accessible to voters and will be responsive to their needs.

Debate

★ PRIMARY ELECTION ★

Fundraiser

Public appearances

Interview with talk radio or newspaper

TV commercial blitz

5 After the primaries, candidates will work hard to unify factions that may have resulted from having multiple candidates within the same party vying for the nomination.

6 In the days leading up to the election, there will be a flurry of commercials and public appearances as candidates work around the clock to sway any undecided voters.

Last-minute public appearances

★ ELECTION DAY ★

Campaign Financing

THE RISING COST of political campaigns and the highly visible role of political action committees (PACs) have led to increasing concern about how elections are financed and how much candidates spend in their efforts to win an office. Many Americans believe that campaign spending is completely out of control and that politicians are devoting increasingly more of their time to raising funds when they should be serving their constituents. Others consider that election expenditures are not out of line when compared to the costs of goods and services in other areas.

Both the amount of money spent on campaigns and the sources of that money are issues that repeatedly come before Congress. Recent proposals for reform have included the following: a cap on spending for House and Senate candidates, federal matching funds for candidates who comply with spending limits, and discounts for mailings and television and radio broadcasts. Political differences are only part of the reason that campaign finance laws, enacted in the 1970s, have not been reformed. There is also concern that campaign finance reforms could once again lead to First Amendment objections or perhaps open a Pandora's box of new, and even more questionable, campaign finance practices.

A Supreme Court ruling in 1976 allowed federal limits to remain in place on contributions to candidates' campaigns but struck down any limits on campaign expenditures by candidates. Limiting political expenditures was deemed to be a violation of the First Amendment rights of candidates and the public. However, the Court did allow the limits on campaign contributions to remain in place in order to protect the integrity of the electoral process.

Candidates for federal office have several legal sources of campaign funds. Presidential candidates can receive federal matching funds from the U.S. treasury. These are financed by the donation checked off on income tax returns. In 1993, this was increased to $3 from $1 for single returns and $6 for joint returns.

Individual citizens are the ultimate source of campaign contributions. Individuals can contribute up to $1,000 per candidate, per election. They can give up to $20,000 per year to a national party committee, and up to $5,000 per year to any other political committee. In total, individuals can give up to $25,000 in political contributions each year. While individuals may (and still do) contribute directly to a campaign, they are increasingly making their political donations through political action committees.

Political action committees have grown rapidly and in effect have filled the void left when federal election laws eliminated "fat cat" donors. PACs are typically organized by business, professionals, labor, or other interest groups to raise funds from their members, stockholders, or employees in order to combine many small donations into larger, and more meaningful, contributions to the candidate(s) of their choice. PACs may contribute up to $5,000 per candidate, per election (primary, runoff, and general elections count as separate elections) provided that they are registered with the Federal Elections Commission (FEC), have at least 50 donors, and contribute to at least five candidates for federal office.

"Soft money" is another source for campaign funds. It, too, is spent to influence the outcome of elections but is not subject to the limitations that apply to direct contributions. Soft money describes funds that are used to indirectly support candidates for political office through efforts to educate voters, get voters registered and to the polls, build party alliances, and set up and administer PACs. Campaign materials such as buttons, bumper stickers, and yard signs used by volunteers can all be paid for with soft money. It is money that is not subject to FEC reporting and disclosure requirements.

In contrast, "hard money" describes money that is accounted for, disclosed, and subject to limitations. Some perceive the existence of soft money as a loophole in current campaign finance law, especially when very large sums (sometimes reaching into six figures) are contributed by a single source, and this has led to calls for regulation or elimination of these funds.

Independent expenditures are those made without consulting with the campaign or candidate. One famous example of the use of independent expenditures occurred in 1988. A group of Californians who supported George Bush for president spent $92,000 on a television ad that publicized then-Governor Michael Dukakis's furlough of Willie Horton, a convicted felon who committed a violent crime while out on furlough. This ad generated a great deal of attention nationwide, focusing as it did on crime and, by implication, race, and became one of the central campaign issues.

The Federal Election Commission was organized in 1975 to monitor federal election laws, including those having to do with the disclosure of campaign contributions and expenditures. The commission is mandated by law to strive for "voluntary compliance" of campaign finance laws. Offenses in reporting or organization are typically dealt with by the FEC unless criminal intent can be proven (which isn't too often).

Criminal cases are pursued by the Department of Justice. In addition to overseeing election laws, the FEC reviews and audits campaign financial data and makes this information available to the public, and registers political action committees. Controversy has surrounded the FEC since its inception, however, primarily because FEC jurisdiction continues to be tightly controlled by Congress—conveying an image of having the fox in charge of the hen house.

Where Do Campaign Contributions Come From?

Political action committees (PACs) typically represent business and interest groups. Overwhelmingly, they contribute to incumbents. PACs contribute to candidates who have supported them in the past and who are likely to be sympathetic to them in the future. While a PAC contribution won't buy a vote, it can buy *access* to the member so that the group's position is more likely to be considered when a critical vote comes up. Some of the largest political action committees (based on 1991–92 contributions to federal candidates) represent the American Medical Association, the National Education Association, the National Rifle Association, Realtors, and the Association of Trial Lawyers.

Individuals might contribute to political campaigns because they especially like a candidate and agree with the candidate's ideology, or in hopes of realizing some form of personal or financial gain. Supporters may donate money directly or perhaps purchase tickets to campaign fundraising events such as a dinner featuring a prominent speaker, or a "birthday party" for the candidate.

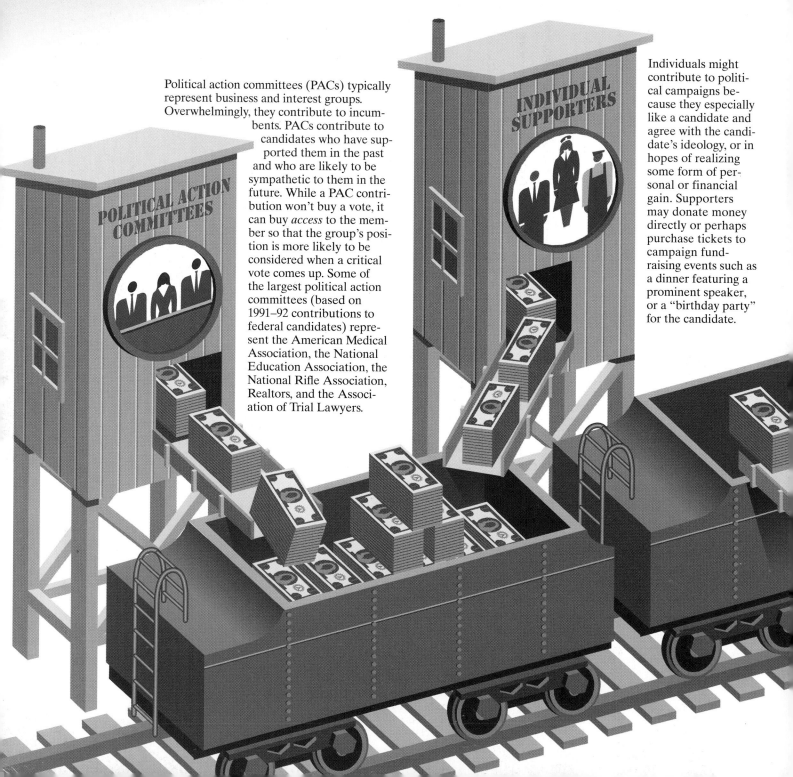

PERSONAL FINANCES

Candidates can contribute to their own campaigns from personal or family resources and from loans. Ross Perot demonstrated just how much attention a candidate could get through the use of personal resources in the 1992 campaign. Presidential candidates who receive federal matching funds can contribute up to $10 million for primary elections and $20 million for the general election. Because congressional candidates do not receive federal matching funds, there is no limit to the amount they can contribute to their own campaign coffers.

PROHIBITED CONTRIBUTIONS

Candidates for federal office cannot accept contributions from national banks, labor unions, corporations, or foreign nationals. Cash (domestic and foreign currency), contributions in amounts of more than $100, and anonymous contributions of more than $50 are also prohibited.

CAMPAIGN EXPRESS

ELECTIONS

PARTY COMMITTEES

Party committees use direct mail and host fund-raising events that often feature celebrities or well-known political figures to attract more contributors. Party committees can give $1,000 or $5,000 per candidate per election, depending on whether they are a multicandidate committee. (A multicandidate committee has at least 50 contributors, has been registered with the FEC for six months or more, and, except for state party committees, contributes to at least five candidates for Federal office.)

CHAPTER

13

Ethics in Congress

SCANDALS INVOLVING OUR elected officials seem to be occurring with increasing frequency, and if one is to believe the evening news, Congress is composed almost exclusively of people who accept bribes, misuse funds, pedal influence, violate campaign finance rules, and engage in sexual exploits worthy of any seamy novel. Repeated reports of scandals—for example, the Keating Five (the investigation of senators who were suspected of accepting political contributions from the head of a failed savings and loan), and the House Bank covering members' overdrafts— reduces not only the credibility of Congress, but our confidence in the institution as a whole.

We rightfully expect our elected officials to conform to the highest ethical standards. But in reality, the incidence of corruption in Congress is probably no more prevalent today than in earlier times. What has changed however, is (1) the public's sensitivity to the appearance of wrongdoing and (2) the likelihood that questionable activities will be exposed by the media, law enforcement agencies, or other members of Congress. Actions that were once ignored or merely winked at are now scrutinized and are likely to be punished in some way.

The founding fathers devised the system of checks and balances, in part, to reduce the likelihood of corruption. However, as we have seen throughout this book, there are many opportunities for individuals and interest groups attempt to influence government—and just as many opportunities for unscrupulousness. Matters are further complicated because of "gray" areas in the rules regarding, for example, allowable sources of income and campaign contributions, taxpayer-funded travel, and use of influence for constituent benefit.

The Constitution states that "each House may determine the Rules of its Proceedings, punish its members for disorderly Behavior, and, with the Concurrence of two thirds, expel a Member." The founding fathers left the details of determining the rules and administering punishments up to Congress. Today, criminal statutes in the U.S. Code of Federal Regulations and codes of ethics in both the House and Senate govern the conduct of members.

Briefly, members are required to disclose their personal finances, income that may be earned outside of Congress is restricted, and there are strict guidelines on how public funds may be used. To reduce the potential for conflicts of interest, the House banned honoraria (fees for speeches, articles, and public appearances) in 1989, and the Senate followed suit in 1991. Book royalties, an issue that contributed to the downfall of the former Speaker of the House, Jim Wright of Texas, have also been a concern for the current Speaker, Newt Gingrich of Georgia; they are permitted provided that no special allowances are made by the publisher simply because the author is a member of Congress.

The Senate Ethics Committee and the House Committee on Standards of Official Conduct are required to investigate allegations of wrong-doing and make recommendations to their respective chambers on whether to discipline a member. These are not popular committees on which to serve!

Members have traditionally been hesitant to pass judgment on their colleagues, but this can vary depending on the severity of the accusations. Legislators often think that a colleague's constituents—the voters—should be the ones to decide whether a member is guilty of wrongdoing. Should a member's actions be downright illegal, the courts will pass judgment.

In many cases, the ethics committee will delay its probe into suspected violations until after an election. If the case has generated considerable attention in the district, voters may oust the accused member—as happened to the 18-term Illinois Democrat Dan Rostenkowski, who was charged with misuse of public funds—thus sparing congressional colleagues the unpleasantness. In the case of Rostenkowski, federal investigators requested that congressional ethics committees delay their investigation so as to not interfere with the federal investigation. It is not unheard of for a member under fire to resign or retire during an ethics investigation (as did former House Speaker Jim Wright) rather than face a further raking over the coals or, ultimately, disciplinary action.

While it may sound as though Congress would, if given their way, pass on the responsibilities for ethics spelled out in the Constitution, keep in mind that not only are members highly loyal to each other (especially within the same party) and Congress as an institution, it is often extremely difficult to determine just what constitutes misuses of power or conflicts of interest.

Should members of Congress be found guilty of misconduct, they may face punishment by their colleagues, the judicial system, or their constituents—or all of these.

There are three ways in which Congress can punish a member. The first, and most severe, is *expulsion,* which requires a two-thirds majority vote. During the Civil War several senators and representatives were expelled for their loyalty to the Confederacy. Since then, only one member of the House has been expelled—though votes for expulsion have been taken a number times in both chambers. Michael J. "Ozzie" Meyers,

Democrat of Pennsylvania, was expelled from the House in 1980 for his involvement in Abscam (an FBI sting operation in which some members were videotaped—and later convicted of—accepting bribes in exchange for using their influence in areas such as obtaining U.S. residency, federal grants, and gambling licenses).

More frequently, Congress *censures* an accused member by conducting a formal hearing before the entire Senate or House. The member stands before the chamber while the transgressions are read aloud. A simple majority vote is necessary to censure a member. As of 1980, House members censured by the House must give up any committee or subcommittee chairmanships they hold. There is an unwritten rule that members convicted of a federal crime should refrain from voting.

A *reprimand* is the mildest form of punishment, as the accused member does not have to stand before congressional colleagues and be publicly humiliated while infringements are discussed and whether to reprimand is voted upon (again a simple majority is required).

Legislators who have been charged with financial corruption (accepting bribes, for example) or any other activity prohibited by federal criminal statutes must go before the courts. However, the Federal Election Commission is responsible for oversight of campaign finance laws and makes its own determination on whether violators should be merely fined, or taken to court.

Constituents are often very harsh critics of their elected official's actions. Jokes about "we know he's a crook, but he's *our* crook" aside, the voters are in a unique position to make or break a political career. Increasingly, constituents are passing judgment on legislator behavior at the polls. A recent example of voters speaking their minds is the 1992 election, when many members who had overdrawn their accounts at the House Bank were defeated—voters were furious at such a blatant example of members of Congress not having to abide to rules that govern the rest of the public.

Gray Areas in Congressional Ethics

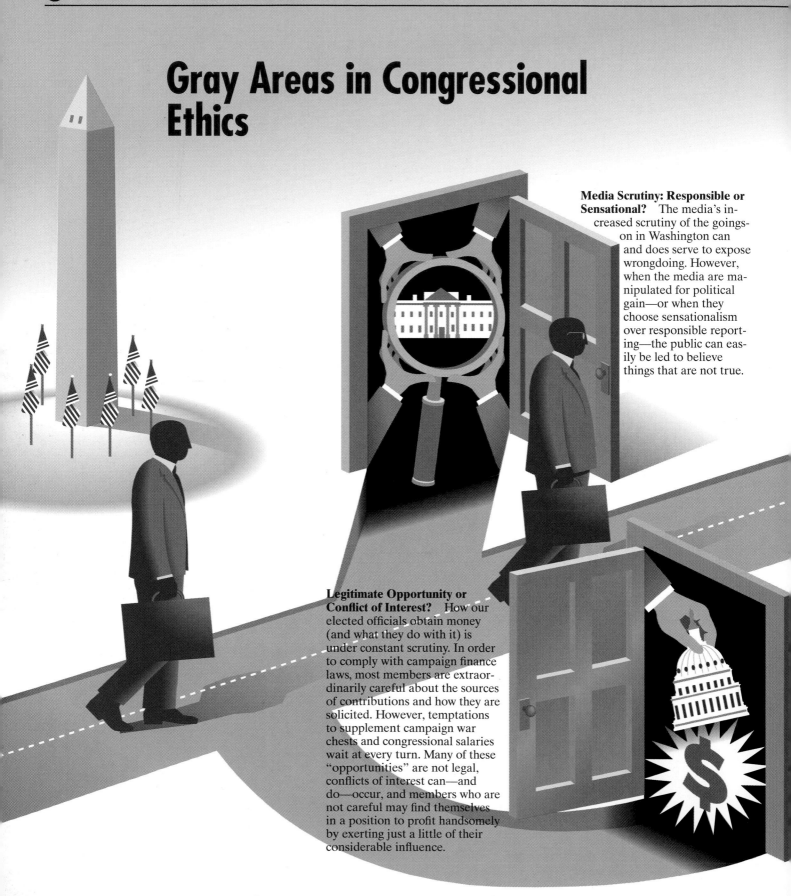

Media Scrutiny: Responsible or Sensational? The media's increased scrutiny of the goings-on in Washington can and does serve to expose wrongdoing. However, when the media are manipulated for political gain—or when they choose sensationalism over responsible reporting—the public can easily be led to believe things that are not true.

Legitimate Opportunity or Conflict of Interest? How our elected officials obtain money (and what they do with it) is under constant scrutiny. In order to comply with campaign finance laws, most members are extraordinarily careful about the sources of contributions and how they are solicited. However, temptations to supplement campaign war chests and congressional salaries wait at every turn. Many of these "opportunities" are not legal, conflicts of interest can—and do—occur, and members who are not careful may find themselves in a position to profit handsomely by exerting just a little of their considerable influence.

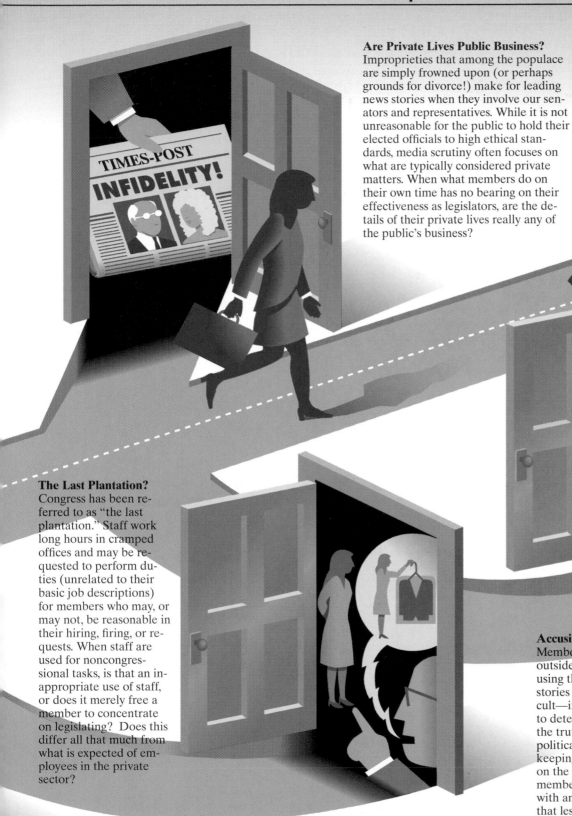

Are Private Lives Public Business?

Improprieties that among the populace are simply frowned upon (or perhaps grounds for divorce!) make for leading news stories when they involve our senators and representatives. While it is not unreasonable for the public to hold their elected officials to high ethical standards, media scrutiny often focuses on what are typically considered private matters. When what members do on their own time has no bearing on their effectiveness as legislators, are the details of their private lives really any of the public's business?

The Last Plantation?

Congress has been referred to as "the last plantation." Staff work long hours in cramped offices and may be requested to perform duties (unrelated to their basic job descriptions) for members who may, or may not, be reasonable in their hiring, firing, or requests. When staff are used for noncongressional tasks, is that an inappropriate use of staff, or does it merely free a member to concentrate on legislating? Does this differ all that much from what is expected of employees in the private sector?

Accusing Others: Truth or Politics?

Members of Congress (and even people outside of Congress) are not above using the media's hunger for political stories for their own gain. It can be difficult—if not impossible—for the public to determine if accusers are exposing the truth or making false accusations for political gain. There is no question that keeping the media's attention focused on the political ramifications of another member's book deal or relationship with an influential businessman means that less time can be devoted to stories on whether the real business of Congress (legislating) is getting done.

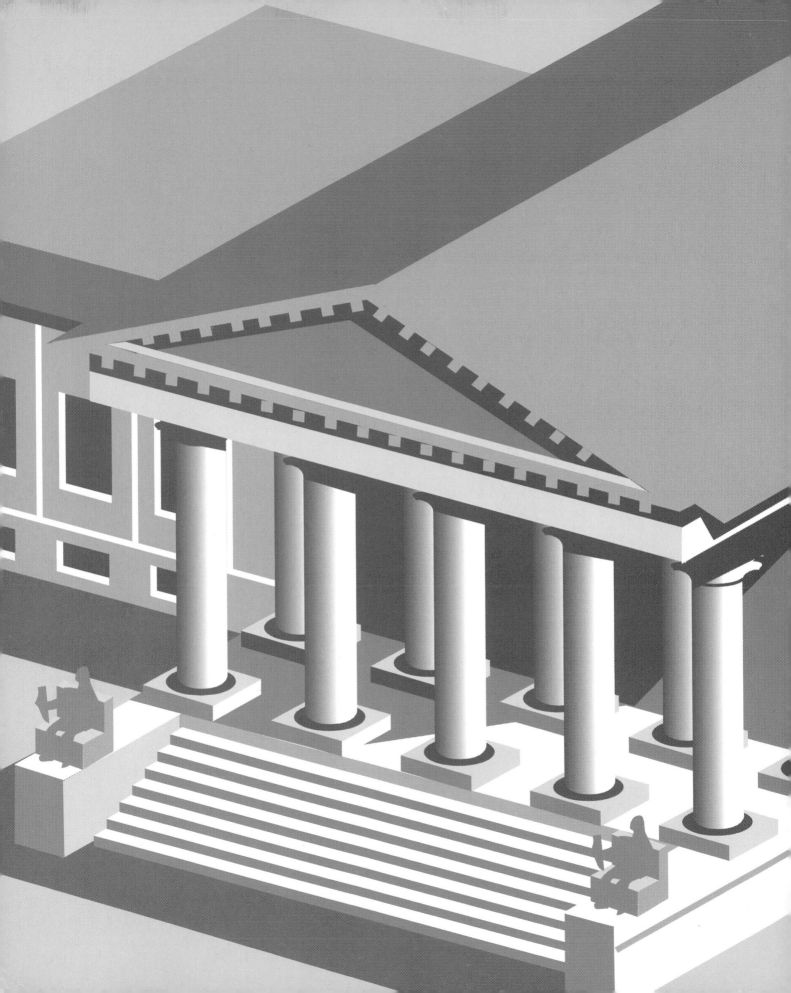

THE JUDICIAL BRANCH

CONTENTS

THE JUDICIAL BRANCH serves to monitor legislation that is developed by Congress and carried out by the executive branch. Because the judicial branch (composed of the Supreme Court and the lower federal courts) serves to keep the other two branches of government from running roughshod over the rights of the people, people tend to view it in a more favorable light than they do either the president or Congress.

Americans have turned increasingly to the courts not only to clarify and explain the intent of laws, but to settle disputes. Virtually every aspect of our lives has been touched upon in some way by the courts—often, when there was no consensus among the public (such as on the issues of racial segregation or abortion).

The types of cases brought before the federal judiciary often mirror changes in the attitudes of the public at large. While the judicial branch is set up to review the fairness of laws in light of the Constitution, the interpretation of Constitutional provisions can change (and has) in light of societal changes, the views of different judges, and even the political climate. In this way, too, courts themselves have become a vehicle for change.

Federal judges are selected and nominated by the president. A simple majority vote of the Senate serves to confirm nominees. Unlike candidates for the presidency and Congress, nominees to the federal bench are not subject to specific constitutional requirements. "Judges…shall hold their Offices during good Behavior." This means for life or until the judge voluntarily resigns or retires. Judges can be impeached, although only seven have been successfully removed from the bench to date.

Judges are in a unique position to interpret legislation and executive action. They can even rule against the other two branches and declare a law or action unconstitutional. However, because federal courts have wide-ranging remedial powers, judges (especially those on the Supreme Court) have been accused by some of overstepping their bounds, of "legislating" rather than merely "judging."

The outline for our federal judiciary is set forth in the Constitution. However, other than vesting power in "one supreme Court," the founding fathers left the establishment of any lower courts, and their structure, to the discretion of Congress.

In addition to the Supreme Court, circuit courts, and district courts, there are "specialty" courts that have limited jurisdiction. For example, all bankruptcy cases go to bankruptcy courts, and military courts hear all actions that fall under the code of military justice.

The Supreme Court is the most visible and glamorous of the constitutional courts. In addition, there are 94 district courts and 13 courts of appeals.

Federal suits nearly always begin in district courts. In fact, most of the work of the federal judiciary is carried out by district courts, which are trial courts for civil and criminal cases under state and federal laws. The courts of appeals cover large geographic areas and are officially called circuit courts, from the days when judges actually "rode the circuit." Appeals from district courts, legislative courts, federal administrative agencies, and independent regulatory commissions are usually resolved in courts of appeals.

The power of judicial review places the courts in a key position to resolve disputes among the three branches of government. The courts evaluate the legislation and actions of the other two branches to determine whether or not they are consistent with the Constitution, and can either oppose or support the president and Congress. Because the Constitution is silent on many topics, there is a great deal of room for a variety of interpretations and opinions by members of the judiciary.

The federal judiciary also arbitrates between the federal government and the states, and through their interpretation of the Constitution, seeks to establish the differences between the rights of individuals and the interests of society as a whole.

The Supreme Court is the most visible of all the federal courts. The number of justices (currently nine) is determined by Congress, however, and not the Constitution. Justices are nominated by the president and confirmed by the Senate in a process that generates considerable interest among the public, for presidents invariably try to put their own ideological stamp on the Supreme Court through their appointments to the bench.

Throughout our history, the Supreme Court has ruled on many cases that continue to affect our lives today. Currently, issues involving cultural, political, and human freedoms have superseded the questions of economic and property rights prevalent in Supreme Court decisions prior to the New Deal. While the abortion issue is one that receives constant media attention, decisions set down by the court have (among other things) guaranteed poor defendants the right to an attorney, ensured that law enforcement officers cannot beat confessions out of their suspects, and guaranteed equality for all regardless of race, sex, or religion.

CHAPTER 14

The Federal Courts: Structure and Jurisdiction

THE FEDERAL COURT system has three tiers. At the lowest level, there are 94 *district courts*. Most federal cases are heard (and decided) in district courts. These cases generally involve straightforward interpretations of the law and rarely result in changes in public policy. The number of district courts in each state and U.S. territory is determined by population, but each state has at least one, and some have as many as four. Also included at this level are the legislative courts, such as the U.S. Court of International Trade and the U.S. Claims Court.

Next are the 13 *courts of appeal* (circuit courts) that serve as intermediate appellate courts. They review decisions of law made by the district courts and cases that result from the actions of government agencies. Courts of appeal are broken down primarily into geographic regions. The District of Columbia has its own court of appeal (which includes the federal government), and there is another court that reviews lower court rulings in cases related to trademarks, patents, and copyrights nationwide. In addition, appeals from some of the federal administrative agencies, such as the Federal Trade Commission, are brought to these courts. While it is possible to appeal a case all the way to the Supreme Court, in most instances, decisions of the courts of appeal are final.

At the top of the federal judicial system is the *Supreme Court*. It is the most powerful court in the federal judicial system—and in the entire country. The Supreme Court's decisions become "the supreme law of the land" because this court is the final rung on the ladder of appellate courts. Cases come to the Supreme Court from the lower federal courts, and from state court systems when a constitutional question or a question of federal law is invoved. The Court has a great deal of control over its own docket and can choose which cases it wishes to hear. If the Court chooses not to hear a case, the decision of the lower court stands.

Every court case begins as a conflict between two (or more) parties. Those involved may be individuals, groups, or governments.

Two types of cases are heard in court—criminal and civil. In *criminal cases*, a prosecutor (representing the government) seeks to punish the defendant (an individual) for violating laws. Governments prosecute in criminal cases because breaking the law is considered to be a crime against society as a whole. *Civil cases* result when there is a dispute between two parties. The plaintiff claims to have suffered some harm, and the defendant is allegedly responsible for causing that harm. The government can bring civil cases to court and can be sued in civil actions.

When private citizens disagree, the case is most often decided at the first level in which it is heard. Often, the losers do not have the time or financial resources needed to mount an appeal. It can take several years for a case to make it all the way to the Supreme Court and be decided there.

A court must have jurisdiction before it can hear a case. Jurisdiction, the authority to hear and decide cases, is granted by statute or in a constitution. Not all courts have jurisdiction over all types of cases.

In both the federal and state court systems, there are courts that handle only specific types of cases (such as taxes and military justice in federal courts and divorce or traffic violations in state courts) and others with *general jurisdiction* that can decide all types of civil and criminal cases. Courts of general jurisdiction usually do not hear cases for which there is a special court.

Courts having *original jurisdiction* are those in which a case is first heard. It is here that trials are conducted and the facts about a case are determined. Courts of original jurisdiction (or, "first instance") include federal district courts and state superior courts as well as county and municipal courts. Most courts are, in fact, courts of original jurisdiction, and most of the nation's judicial business begins, and ends, in these courts.

In contrast are courts that have *appellate jurisdiction*. These courts act as reviewing courts and hear cases brought to them on appeal from lower courts. At the state level, the appeal process generally ends in the state's highest court. The only court in which to appeal a decision of a state high court is the U.S. Supreme Court. However, one cannot always appeal to the U.S. Supreme Court from a state supreme court. In order to do so, the case must involve a question of federal law or the U.S. Constitution.

Each state is permitted to design its court system according to its own needs. Most states follow a structure similar to that of the federal judiciary. Generally states have two levels of trial courts, the lower for criminal cases involving minor crimes, and the upper for civil cases and major criminal cases. In the middle, states have an intermediate court of appeal. At the top of the state judiciary is a state supreme court or differently-named equivalent.

Nearly all of the cases that enter a state's court system are resolved in the court of original jurisdiction. Should one of the parties involved be unhappy with the trial's outcome, the person can appeal.

Despite the division between what constitutes a state matter and what constitutes a federal matter, some cases that begin in a state court end up in federal court. Often cases of this nature involve a state statute and a constitutional right, or a combination of state and federal laws.

While one cannot dispute the broader importance of Supreme Court and appellate court decisions that develop (and revise) our social politics and legal precedents, it is not surprising that decisions made in lower courts have a more direct and immediate impact on our daily lives. As members of the public, we are far more likely to be involved in disputes concerning specific issues than we are in decisions that would necessitate the reinterpretation of federal laws.

Structure of the Federal Court System

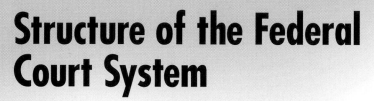

The U.S. Tax Court decides cases involving the over- or underpayment of taxes.

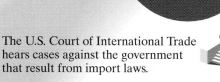

U.S. COURTS OF APPEALS

Ninety-four district courts try and decide most of the federal cases. Each state and U.S. territory has at least one district court (the number is determined by population), and some of the larger states have as many as four.

The U.S. Court of International Trade hears cases against the government that result from import laws.

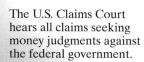

The U.S. Claims Court hears all claims seeking money judgments against the federal government.

THE SUPREME COURT OF THE UNITED STATES

There are 13 U.S. courts of appeals (also known as "circuit courts"). Courts of appeals also hear cases from many of the federal agencies.

U.S. COURTS OF APPEALS FOR THE FEDERAL CIRCUIT

The U.S. Court of Appeals for the Federal Circuit hears appeals regarding patent and trademark cases, and from such special courts as the courts of federal claims, international trade, and veterans appeals.

U.S. COURTS OF MILITARY APPEALS

The U.S. Court of Military Appeals considers court-martial convictions of certain kinds such as death penalty convictions from military courts and petitions from those who receive sentences of more than one year in prison.

The U.S. Court of Veterans Appeals reviews decisions made by the Board of Veterans Appeals.

The Courts of Military Review serve as intermediate courts of appeal and consider decisions made by courts of the Army, Navy/Marine Corps, Air Force, and Coast Guard. The president, as commander-in-chief, is the final arbiter for military appeals.

Jurisdiction of the Federal Courts

EQUAL·JUSTICE·UNDER·LAW

THE SUPREME COURT

The Supreme Court of the United States has *original jurisdiction* (which means the case begins in the Supreme Court) over controversies between the U.S. and a state, two or more states, a state and a citizen of a different state (only if the state initiates action, otherwise the case must begin in state court), and involving foreign ambassadors or other diplomats. Cases in which the Supreme Court has original jurisdiction are extremely rare.

The Supreme Court has *appellate jurisdiction* (which means the case began in a lower court) from lower federal constitutional courts, most federal legislative courts, and the highest state court having jurisdiction when the case involves a federal constitutional issue.

U.S. COURTS OF APPEALS

U.S. courts of appeals have no original jurisdiction and *hear only appeals* from a variety of courts, independent regulatory commissions, and some federal agencies and departments.

U.S. DISTRICT COURTS

U.S. district courts have original jurisdiction over cases involving questions of criminal or civil law, or constitutional questions of federal law; and in cases in which the defendant and plaintiff are from different states and the amount being sued for exceeds $50,000. In addition, these courts review actions of certain administrative agencies and departments and any other cases that may be assigned by Congress.

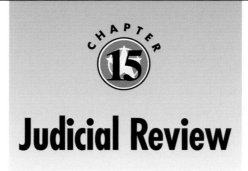

Judicial Review

LIKE SO MANY aspects of our government today, the power of judicial review is not spelled out in the Constitution—although the importance of having a political arbiter is implied. Judicial review was first established as a power of the courts in the famous 1803 case, *Marbury v. Madison* (in which William Marbury was denied a judicial appointment by Thomas Jefferson's Secretary of State, James Madison—the Court ruled in favor of Marbury). Throughout the nearly 200 years since *Marbury v. Madison*, the incidence of judicial decisions that have overturned executive and legislative actions has steadily increased. While the wording of constitutional provisions has remained unchanged, the meaning of these provisions has been (and continues to be) revised as they are applied to new situations.

We commonly think of judicial review as the courts' power to declare laws and government acts unconstitutional. However, judicial review also means that the courts will stand behind government and uphold laws they find to be constitutional.

The power of judicial review places the courts in a unique position to resolve disputes among the three branches of government, between the federal government and the states, and, when necessary, to differentiate between the rights of individuals and the interests of society as a whole.

Through the use of judicial review, federal courts have had an impact on virtually every aspect of our society. In fact, the courts often become political players when they are forced to resolve issues on which there is no national consensus (such as in the cases of racial segregation or abortion) and passions run high on both sides. Judges are therefore extraordinarily powerful, for whenever they interpret the Constitution, or significantly expand the scope of existing laws, they make policy.

The judicial branch truly does have a great deal of autonomy, but it is important that judges be insulated from the rest of the political process so that they can defend—without concern for political repercussion—groups whose concerns might otherwise go unheard by the legislative and executive branches. Constitutional provisions guarantee judicial independence by specifying that justices are appointed for life and cannot have their salaries lowered while in office (and thus cannot be fired or subject to a pay cut should they make an unpopular decision).

There are both supporters and detractors of the judiciary's power to rule actions of the president and Congress unconstitutional. Those who consider the concept of judicial review to be undemocratic cite the fact that the judges who have the power to determine what is and is not in accordance with the Constitution are not accountable to the public in the same way as are elected officials. On the other side of the coin are those who consider the power of judicial review essential to ensure that the rights of all (but especially the minority) are safeguarded.

Despite the significance of the power of judicial review, only a small fraction of the thousands of laws enacted by Congress and the president have been struck down by the courts. More often, it is the state laws that are declared null and void because they tend to reflect more narrow interests and are thus more likely to be in conflict with the U.S. Constitution. However, the concept of judicial checks is an integral part of the legislative process, and both Congress and the states make an effort to avoid enacting laws that are likely to be struck down.

While the judicial branch can make rulings, it must rely upon others, mainly the executive branch, for enforcement, and enforcing the compliance of states (especially when carrying out court orders) often requires the appropriation of funds by the legislative branch. For example, Presidents Eisenhower and Kennedy had to send troops to several southern states in order to enforce court orders to desegregate public schools and universities.

Notwithstanding the courts' considerable inherent and implied powers, the judiciary remains subject to some executive and legislative branch control.

Over the long term, presidents can mold the courts to a certain degree through their appointments to the federal bench. However, in the case of the Supreme Court (whose rulings tend to have the most far-reaching impact), a president usually has the opportunity to make only a very few appointments—if any—during his term of office.

Congress can reverse judicial decisions by either amending the Constitution (of course, amendments must be ratified by three-quarters of the states) or passing new legislation. Amending the U.S. Constitution is not an easy task, however, and it is understood that every disagreement with a Supreme Court ruling should not result in a constitutional amendment. In fact, every amendment proposed since 1971 has failed somewhere along the way—usually not even getting out of Congress. In recent years, proposed amendments that would have reversed court decisions (on the issues of prayer in schools and abortion, for example) have met with failure. Congress has been a great deal more successful in reversing court decisions through revising objectionable legislation in order to address the judiciary's concerns.

While Congress also has the power to change the structure of the lower federal courts, limit the Supreme Court's jurisdiction, and impeach judges, these "checks" are resorted to only rarely.

Independent Counsel

Provisions for the appointment of independent counsel (also called "special prosecutor") are relatively new. The need for investigators who were not beholden to the executive branch became evident during the Watergate era, when the attorney general and his assistant resigned rather than fire the special prosecutor Archibald Cox for demanding the oval office tapes.

TIMES-POST

IRAN-CONTRA INVESTIGATED

More recently, an independent counsel was appointed to investigate the role of White House officials and Lt. Col. Oliver North in the sale of arms to Iran. During the Iran-Contra hearings, the constitutionality of the special prosecutor law was being challenged. Administration concerns that having Congress determine the scope of an investigation infringed upon the president's power to enforce the law were overruled by the Supreme Court in the 1988 *Morrison v. Olson* decision.

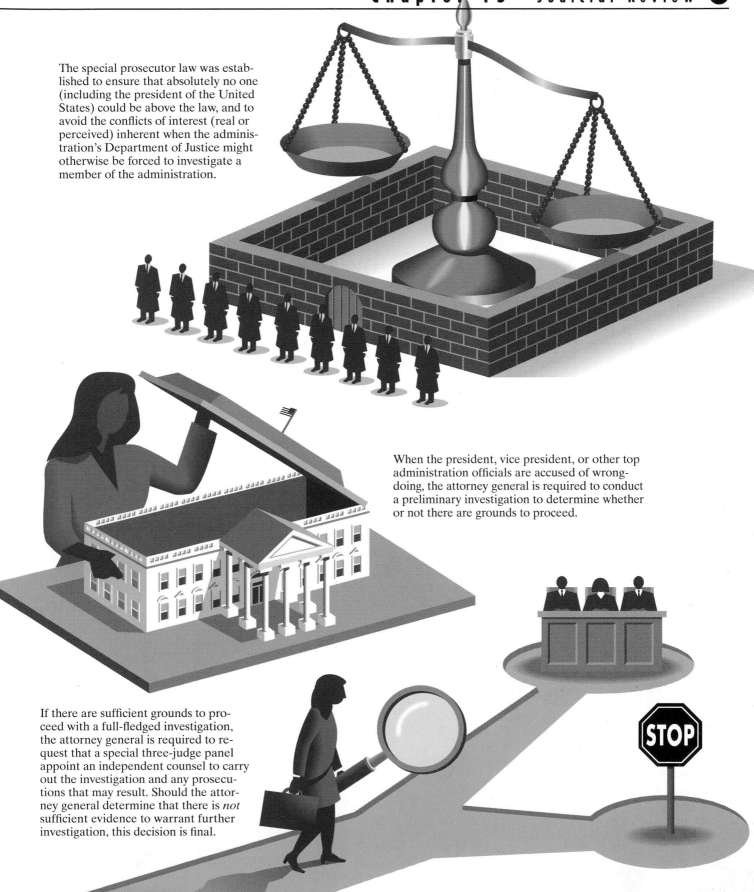

The special prosecutor law was established to ensure that absolutely no one (including the president of the United States) could be above the law, and to avoid the conflicts of interest (real or perceived) inherent when the administration's Department of Justice might otherwise be forced to investigate a member of the administration.

When the president, vice president, or other top administration officials are accused of wrongdoing, the attorney general is required to conduct a preliminary investigation to determine whether or not there are grounds to proceed.

If there are sufficient grounds to proceed with a full-fledged investigation, the attorney general is required to request that a special three-judge panel appoint an independent counsel to carry out the investigation and any prosecutions that may result. Should the attorney general determine that there is *not* sufficient evidence to warrant further investigation, this decision is final.

STOP

Judges as Activists

These three factors have contributed significantly to increased opportunities for judicial activism:

Federal courts make policy on both large and small issues, and while the Supreme Court is not the only court that interprets laws and makes policy, its decisions are the most far-reaching.

Gaining access to the courts has become increasingly easy for both groups and individuals through class-action suits, "friend of the court" briefs, and the ongoing efforts of such private groups as the National Association for the Advancement of Colored People (NAACP) and the American Civil Liberties Union (ACLU). The more cases heard, the greater the opportunity for change.

Laws passed by Congress are often so ambiguous as to give judges quite a bit of room for interpretation.

Court decisions often are broad in scope and thus have an impact upon large categories of people such as women, people with disabilities, or even prisoners.

Should judges go too far in advancing change, they are likely to lose credibility with the public and face chastisement from Congress.

Judicial activism is not without controversy. Those in favor of judicial activism believe that it is the responsibility of the federal courts to correct injustices when Congress and the president (or states) fail to do so, because courts are the institutions of last resort. Opponents believe that policy making should be left to elected officials, who have access to greater resources and expertise and who must be accountable to the public.

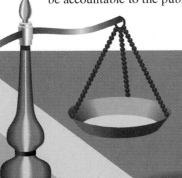

CHAPTER
16

The Supreme Court

THE SUPREME COURT is the most visible, glamorous, and powerful judicial body in the nation. The Court's role in government is a special one, for as the ultimate interpreter of the U.S. Constitution, its decisions serve not only to safeguard justice, but also to shape our government's domestic policy.

Since 1869, the Court has been composed of one chief justice and eight associate justices. Over the years, there have been as few as five justices (1789) and as many as ten (1863). Each justice is assisted in reviewing petitions, studying cases, and writing opinions by three or four law clerks, who are usually recent graduates of the nation's top law schools.

All federal judges are nominated by the president and confirmed by a simple majority vote in the Senate. While the Constitution does not specify what qualifications judges must have—not all judges have prior judicial experience—it is generally understood that nominees are lawyers and, in the case of the Supreme Court, members of the president's political party.

In the search for Supreme Court candidates, the Department of Justice generally draws from lower federal courts, state courts, or the federal government. Likely prospects are then recommended to the president by the attorney general. Nominees may be selected on the basis of ideological views and political experience and, to a lesser degree, because of personal friendships or favors. During his presidency, Ronald Reagan strongly emphasized political views, and his administration sought out candidates who had proven that their stands on controversial issues were conservative. At other times, nominees to the Supreme Court have been chosen in order to provide representation for groups who did not yet have a member on the court. As the nation grew, for example, presidents were pressured to select nominees from western states. Over the years nominees have included blacks, women, Jews, and Catholics as presidents sought the support of diverse groups of people.

Once the name of a nominee has been made public, the nomination process usually takes the following course: The American Bar Association's Committee on the Federal Judiciary typically prepares a report, evaluating the individual being considered, for the Senate Judiciary Committee's hearings. Hearings on candidates to the bench are similar to hearings on legislative topics. The

Judiciary Committee invites both written and oral testimony, and senators question the nominee about his or her judicial philosophy. Political allies and opponents and interest groups all lobby members of the committee intensively. Those for and against try to ascertain what kind of decisions the individual might make on the bench if confirmed. Should a nominee make it through the hearing process (nominations that become politically volatile may be withdrawn), the committee will vote to either accept or reject the nominee. If the committee votes to accept, then the nomination is brought before the full Senate for a vote.

Nominees for federal judgeships may be rejected for a variety of reasons. Supreme Court nominees have been rejected for (among other things) political reasons, concerns about questionable financial dealings or personal conduct, a record of opposing important social reforms like civil rights, and simply lack of merit.

The Supreme Court is in session from early October through the end of June. During this time, the justices study case briefs, hear oral arguments in the courtroom, discuss their findings in private conference with their colleagues, and develop opinions.

Each year, the Court is asked to review approximately 7,000 decisions from lower federal courts and the state courts. While all of the cases submitted are reviewed, the Court usually agrees to hear oral arguments on only about 85 to 100. In a few cases (usually less than 100) the Court may simply affirm or reverse a lower court's decision without hearing oral arguments. All other petitions for review are refused.

Cases having straightforward answers rarely reach the Supreme Court. Occasionally, however, the Court may decide to revise or reverse an existing decision. Decisions made by the Supreme Court can be expected to have an impact on the entire legal system.

In order to reach their decisions, the justices meet in complete secrecy to discuss (or argue) the cases that they have heard. The chief justice usually states his views first and can often exercise considerable influence in shaping the debate. He is then followed by each of the other justices in order of seniority. After the cases have been debated, the justices vote, and all votes are recorded in the docket book. In order to decide a case, a majority of the justices must agree. Should there be a tie (which can occur if one of the justices is absent or disqualifies him- or herself from the case), the lower court decision remains standing.

The Court traditionally issues a written opinion that explains their decision. If the chief justice votes with the majority, he either writes the opinion himself or assigns it to another. Should the chief justice side with the minority, the senior justice voting with the majority will make the assignment. In roughly 25 percent of the cases, the vote is unanimous. More often, a case will produce concurring and dissenting opinions. A concurring opinion is in agreement with the result arrived at by the majority, but for different reasons. Dissenting opinions are those held by justices in the minority.

While most Supreme Court decisions are complied with, there have been times when unpopular rulings on emotionally charged issues were defied and the justices severely criticized. A noteworthy example of this occurred after the 1954 school integration ruling *Brown v. Board of Education.*

Many states (especially those in the south) strongly resisted the mandate to integrate schools. In 1957 Governor Orval Faubus used the Arkansas National Guard to prevent nine black students from entering Central High School in Little Rock. President Dwight D. Eisenhower was forced to send in the U.S. Army to quell the angry mob and ensure that the students could enter and leave the school safely. Federal troops had to be dispatched again by President John F. Kennedy to curb strong resistance to integration on the campuses of the University of Mississippi in 1962 and the University of Alabama in 1963.

Not surprisingly, there have been attempts by Congress to restrict the Court's power over the years—mostly to no avail. Critics have rejected nominees, enacted legislation postponing the Court's session (to delay decisions in controversial cases), and proposed revoking the Court's authority to hear certain types of cases.

Throughout our history, Supreme Court decisions have served as a vehicle for change in our country. While justices are not legislators, Court decisions have had a significant impact on public policy in many areas, as we'll see in Chapter 17. In fact, the kinds of cases brought to the courts often reflect changes in public attitudes and more often than not concern our basic freedoms.

How Cases Are Brought before the Supreme Court

It is not easy to have your day in the Supreme Court. Most of the applications for Supreme Court review of a case are rejected, legal costs can run high, and settling a matter in federal court may take many years. Disputes that do reach the Supreme Court typically concern broad issues and fundamental questions involving the Constitution or federal law.

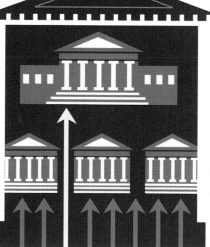

The Supreme Court has considerable control over its own docket, and thus over which cases it will hear. In order for a case to be reviewed, a minimum of four justices must agree that the case merits the Court's attention. Comparatively few cases are ever heard by the Supreme Court. As a result, lower federal courts have substantial power in establishing policy because they serve as the court of last resort for the majority of cases.

There are a number of ways in which a case can come before the Supreme Court. One is when a case is within the Court's original jurisdiction. As we saw in Chapter 14, cases between the federal government and a state, two or more states, or a state and citizen of a different state, or cases involving diplomats or other foreign ambassadors are all within the Supreme Court's original jurisdiction. Cases of original jurisdiction account for only a small number of the Court's decisions.

Most cases heard by the Court result from the granting of a *writ of certiorari* (which, roughly translated, means "to make more certain"), for which a litigant who loses a case in a lower court may petition. If four of the nine justices (not a majority, but a substantial number) consider the case to be worthy of review or find that it might not have been satisfactorily resolved by the lower courts, a writ is granted. Should the Court decline to review a case, it does not have to give its reasons.

Cases brought to the Supreme Court from state supreme courts, through a writ of certiorari, must raise a substantial federal question. Cases that qualify for appeal in the Supreme Court include instances when a right guaranteed by the Constitution is denied by a state, or when a state law is found to be in conflict with federal law.

CHAPTER

Landmark Supreme Court Cases

SUPREME COURT RULINGS have had a tremendous impact on the development of our society. When the nation was young, challenges to the Constitution were relatively few and far between. Early decisions in many cases contributed to the structure and organization of the fledgling United States. As subjects that were of concern to U.S. citizens changed over the years, the Court was required to make rulings on an ever widening variety of issues.

The decisions for the cases discussed on the following pages were not made in a vacuum. History—in the form of wars, the industrial revolution, westward expansion, and the enactment of constitutional amendments, for example—often came into play, and gave rise to circumstances that led to new cases. Views on the roles of women and the rights of minorities changed drastically. Often, rulings were made on a number of cases that lead up to the decisions we now consider to be turning points. In addition, it is not unusual for the Court to revisit issues left unanswered in previous cases or to reverse or clarify an earlier decision.

In the years leading up to and encompassing World War II, the push for patriotism clashed with individual rights to freedom of speech. In 1940 (in *Minersville School District v. Gobitis*) the Court ruled eight to one that individual religious beliefs, such as those held by the children of Jehovah's Witnesses, were not violated by a school requirement that the children stand with their school class and salute the flag. Newspapers nationwide condemned the decision, and there were also incidences of violence against Jehovah's Witnesses by fanatical patriots. This decision was reversed in 1943 (*West Virginia State Board of Education v. Barnette*). Not only had the makeup of the Court changed during the intervening years, but a board of education that expelled students for failing to salute and pledge allegiance to the flag provided the perfect opportunity to overturn the *Gobitis* decision.

In 1963, the Court determined that Bible-reading in public schools was a violation of the First Amendment *(School District of Abington Township, Pa. v. Schempp)* because by permitting reading of the Bible or recitation of the Lord's Prayer in public schools, the government would, to a certain degree, be promoting Christianity. However, the separation of church and state continues to be hotly debated. Members of the "religious right" such as Senator Jesse Helms and the

Reverend Jerry Falwell, founder of "the Moral Majority" are constantly working for passage of legislation that would provide for prayer (more palatably termed "a moment of silence") in public schools. Should they ever succeed in their efforts to enact legislation of this order, it is reasonable to assume that it will not take long for such a law to be overturned by the Supreme Court.

Two highly visible cases, *Gideon v. Wainright* in 1963 and *Miranda v. Arizona* in 1966, granted important protections to those accused of crimes. Clarence E. Gideon studied law while in prison and argued to the Supreme Court that, by virtue of the right to counsel guaranteed by the Sixth Amendment (applicable only to federal cases), he was entitled to be represented by legal counsel. While Gideon was incorrect in his assumption that state court defendants were also entitled to legal counsel—which he had not had at his trial—the Supreme Court agreed with Gideon and ruled in his favor, holding that indigent defendants in state and federal courts are entitled to have an attorney represent them. The Court's determination that everyone is entitled to legal counsel has forever changed our criminal justice system.

Ernesto Miranda, whose name has become a household word, was sent to prison after being convicted of kidnapping and rape. His lawyer appealed the case on the grounds that Miranda's Fifth Amendment rights had been violated because he had been forced to incriminate himself during the police interrogation. In addition, he was not informed that he did not have to respond to police questions, or that anything he did say could be used against him in court. The Supreme Court ruled in favor of Miranda (who was convicted again in the retrial). The majority opinion set forth by Chief Justice Earl Warren resulted in what we refer to today as the Miranda Rights.

The nation's changing views on the roles of blacks in society is illustrated by a number of Supreme Court rulings. For example, in 1857 blacks were considered to be nothing more than property. A slave named Dred Scott was taken by his master to Illinois and other federal territories in which slavery was prohibited, before finally settling in Missouri. Dred Scott tried to win his freedom by basing his suit on the state constitution of Illinois and the federal laws governing the Louisiana Territory, both of which prohibited slavery, but the Supreme Court considered the issue in *Scott v. Sanford* to be the slave owner's property rights, not the civil rights of the slave. The Court ruled against Dred Scott.

Thirty years after the Civil War had ended, Jim Crow laws served to continue discrimination against blacks by whites. The "separate but equal" philosophy that the Court upheld in *Plessy v. Ferguson* (1896) was finally overturned in the 1954 decision

Brown v. Board of Education, when the Court ruled that separate but equal facilities did not meet the Fourteenth Amendment's requirements of equal protection under the law. While the language of the amendment had not changed at all between the years of 1896 and 1954, the Court's interpretation had changed drastically. Eventually, the Court had to strike a balance between promoting opportunities for minorities and instances of "reverse discrimination" as in the 1978 case *University of California Regents v. Bakke.* Allan Bakke was denied admission by a medical school that chose to accept less qualified minority applicants in order to meet self-imposed admissions quotas. The Court determined that race can be only one factor among the many considered when determining which applicants will be accepted or rejected.

The changing role of women in our society has been reflected in—and enhanced by—a number of Court rulings. In *Muller v. Oregon*, 1908, a woman's role as a mother and the need to safeguard her health as producer and nurturer for future generations of Americans were cited as justification for different workplace laws (in this case, the maximum hours of work allowed per day) for women and men. Nearly thirty years later, the Court ruled in *West Coast Hotel Co. v. Parrish* that a state law mandating a minimum wage for women and minors was valid. This decision is considered by many to be the beginning of a more equal role for women in the workplace—a triumph for social justice and the early feminist movement.

No other Supreme Court ruling (except perhaps that of *Brown v. Board of Education*), has drawn as much criticism as *Roe v. Wade.* In 1973, the Court determined that "liberty," as used in the Fourteenth Amendment, includes the right of women to be free from government interference in the decision of whether or not to have an abortion. The Court made no attempt to resolve the extraordinarily difficult question of when life begins. However, it did attempt to balance a woman's right to privacy with the interest of the state in protecting the unborn.

Landmark Supreme Court Cases and Their Places in U.S. History

1803
Marbury v. Madison: This case began as a relatively small dispute over the delay of a commission to the federal judiciary by Thomas Jefferson's secretary of state, James Madison. It is the first time in which the Supreme Court exercised its power of judicial review to declare acts of Congress or the president unconstitutional.

1816
Martin v. Hunter's Lessee: The Court over-turned a Virginia judge's ruling that each state should decide for itself what the Constitution meant—and upheld the right of the U.S. Supreme Court to hear cases of this nature and overturn decisions made by state courts.

1819
McCulloch v. Maryland: Upheld Congress's power to establish a national bank and ruled that states cannot tax federal banks.

1857
Scott v. Sandford: Blacks were held to be property, not citizens, and as such could not be granted the rights and privileges granted to citizens of the U.S.

1896
Plessy v. Ferguson: Segregation of public facilities was not unconstitutional, provided that facilities for blacks and whites were substantially equal.

1787 The Constitution of the United States was adopted.

1793 Eli Whitney invented the cotton gin to mechanically separate cotton seeds from the fibers.

1812–14 War of 1812

1845–48 Mexican-American War

1861–65 Civil War

1865 Slavery was outlawed by the Thirteenth Amendment.

1870 The Fifteenth Amendment granted nonwhite men the right to vote.

1961

Mapp v. Ohio: Evidence obtained without a search warrant is not admissible in court as that violates the search and seizure provisions of the Fourth Amendment.

1954

Brown v. Board of Education: Served as the beginning of school desegregation by reversing an 1896 ruling permitting "separate but equal" facilities. Separate but equal facilities had been found to violate the Fourteenth Amendment's requirement for equal protection under the law.

1940

Minersville School District v. Gobitis: Court ruled that a school district can require students to salute the flag regardless of their individual beliefs. In this case, the Gobitis children were Jehovah's Witnesses.

1908

Muller v. Oregon: Upheld a state law prohibiting women from working for more than 10 hours a day. The physical well-being of women, it was noted, must be protected to ensure the "strength and vigor of the race." Because of differences in men and women, different laws regarding them were justified.

1937

West Coast Hotel Co. v. Parrish: Not only were state minimum wage laws upheld, this case served as the beginning of a more equal role for women in the workplace.

1939–45
World War II

1935

Congress passed the Fair Labor Standards Act which prohibited child labor, and established minimum wages and maximum hours.

1925

John T. Scopes was prosecuted for teaching evolution in the famous "Monkey Trial."

1920

Women were granted the right to vote by the Nineteenth Amendment.

1914-18
World War I

Landmark Supreme Court Cases and Their Places in U.S. History

1962
Engel v. Vitale:
Requiring students in public schools to recite a prayer violates the First Amendment's "establishment clause."

1963
Gideon v. Wainright:
Guaranteed that an attorney will be provided by the state should a defendant be unable to afford to hire one.

1965
Griswold v. Connecticut:
The use of contraceptives by married couples is protected by the right to privacy guaranteed by the Fourteenth Amendment.

1966
Miranda v. Arizona:
Safeguarded against self-incrimination by requiring that police advise a suspect in custody of his rights to remain silent and have legal counsel before questioning is begun.

1973
Roe v. Wade: This case secured the right of a woman to obtain an abortion under most conditions and limited the ability of government to regulate abortion.

1964 Congress passed the Civil Rights Act prohibiting segregation in public places and discriminatory hiring practices.

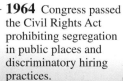

1994
Dolan v. City of Tigard: A city cannot require that private property be given to the city in exchange for building permit approval. This violates the Fifth Amendment.

1986
Ford v. Wainwright: Court determined that the Constitution forbids executing insane prisoners.

1984
New York v. Quarles: Granted an exception to *Miranda* by allowing evidence obtained without advising a suspect of his or her *Miranda* rights to be used in court when the evidence was obtained in the face of an immediate threat to public safety.

1976
Regents of the University of California v. Bakke: Made reverse discrimination in order to meet quotas illegal.

1972
Congress passed the Equal Rights Amendment providing equality for women in all areas. It was never ratified by the necessary three-fourths of the states.

Introducing the Expanded Line of Lavishly Illustrated
"How It Works" Books from Ziff-Davis Press.

ISBN: 1-56276-228-1
Price: $19.95

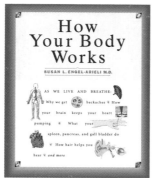

ISBN: 1-56276-231-1
Price: $19.95

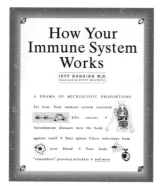

ISBN: 1-56276-233-8
Price: $19.95

ISBN: 1-56276-232-X
Price: $19.95

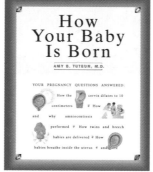

ISBN: 1-56276-239-7
Price: $19.95

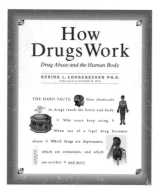

ISBN: 1-56276-241-9
Price: $19.95

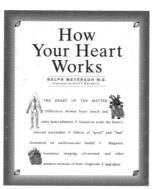

ISBN: 1-56276-238-9
Price: $19.95

This fall, Ziff-Davis Press raises health and science books to an art form with an exciting expansion of the "How It Works" concept that sold over 800,000 copies in its first 18 months.

Why do people love "How it Works"? It's easy to see. Self-contained layouts place an entire topic before the reader's eyes all at once on a set of facing pages. Dramatic, full-color graphics invite them to explore at their own pace. It's a concept so simple, so natural, you'd think it has been done before. It hasn't. Not like this.

How did we pull this off? We auditioned hundreds of authors to find the chosen few who know their stuff and can put it in writing. Backing them up are consulting editors who are equally expert in their field and gifted illustrators who combine topic knowledge with a passion for presentation.

Who reads "How It Works"? Everyone who ever felt too intimidated to ask a doctor a question. Everyone who ever marveled at the miracle of childbirth. Everyone who ever lost a picnic to an unforecast hailstorm. In fact, just about everyone.

Watch for many more subjects in the months ahead!
Available at all fine bookstores, or by calling 1-800-688-0448, ext. 261.

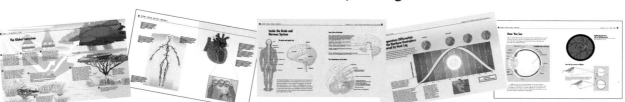

ZIFF-DAVIS
ZD
PRESS